RESTORE YOUR WOODEN BOAT

HOW TO DO IT, BY THOSE WHO'VE DONE IT

RESTORE YOUR WOODEN BOAT

HOW TO DO IT, BY THOSE WHO'VE DONE IT

EDITED BY STAN GRAYSON

DEVEREUX BOOKS
Marblehead, MA

Copyright © 2006 by Devereux Books

Published by Devereux Books
PO Box 503
Marblehead, MA 01945

Internet address: www.devereuxbooks.com

Library of Congress Cataloging in Publication Data

Restore Your Wooden Boat: how to do it by those who've done it / edited by Stan Grayson
        p. cm.
ISBN: 1-928862-11-X (alk. paper)
   Boats and boating – Conservation and restoration. I. Grayson, Stan, 1945-

   VM149.R46   2006
   623.8'207-dc22

Design by Paige Davis, Fish Tank Media

Printed in the United States of America

On the Cover: the restoration of a Winter Harbor Knockabout eventually led Thad Danielson into fulltime boat building and restoration. Thad is the proprietor of Redds Pond Boatworks in Marblehead, Massachusetts, where he restores and builds wooden boats of all sorts. The one seen here is a Concordia Sloop Boat designed by Pete Culler. (Photography by Stan Grayson.)

On the Back Cover: the 1952 Chris-Craft Sportsman was restored by Russ Ballenger who took the picture. The boat is the subject of Chapter 2.

Table of Contents

Introduction

This is a book about how a variety of wooden boat owners restored their boats within limited budgets, and emerged from the process having grown and become enriched in ways both tangible and somehow indefinable. Every one of them reported that the process was a life-enhancing experience. Several of the authors reported that, after being initially "scared off" by reading books written by acknowledged experts, they had gained a new appreciation for what an inspired amateur could accomplish — especially if they didn't let "official" methods "get in the way." Others, however, found specific books to be so helpful that they referred to them time and again. Ultimately, perhaps the most common trait shared by these authors is a willingness to confront a problem, develop a solution adapted to one's own ability, and then persevere steadily until the desired result is achieved.

Assembling this cast of contributors presented a challenge. The basic goal was to present a variety of boat types that had been built with a variety of construction methods. That's why you'll find vessels that range from a rowing semi-dory, a tiny outboard pram, outboard and inboard runabouts, sailboats, and a big power cruiser. Construction methods include lapstrake, glued-seam planking, plywood, and traditional plank-on-frame, among others. As a group, these authors reported learning that there may not be a right or wrong way to accomplish a given task — just the way that works for one who must adapt to specific tools, work space, and experience. Want to learn how to create a rubrail of varying radii and bevels when you really don't know how? Read on.

I was much aided during the planning stages for this book by the "Launchings" section that is such an inspirational part of each issue of *WoodenBoat* magazine. While quite a number of potential contributors were contacted during the book's planning stage, for one reason or another, it was those who'd appeared first in the magazine who ultimately proved to have the interest, discipline, and ability to share their experiences in words and pictures. A few brought extensive woodworking experience to their projects and, absent that background, it is frankly hard to imagine how they would have otherwise tackled their projects. For others, however, their boat's restoration was the first such task they had ever undertaken. Perhaps the key message here is that, given willpower and desire, you might surprise yourself by what you achieve.

Although the boats discussed here are each

unique, the challenges they posed and the methods used to meet those challenges often share common threads. Certain products and tools were exceptionally useful to several of the authors. More than one discovered the goodness of a ready supply of clean cans. Brushes for varnishing? Some used disposable foam brushes and others the "real McCoy" with equally satisfactory results. Not to be overlooked is the occasional availability of friends who can supply the needed muscle power to flip over a hull or accomplish some other weighty task. Among the most important messages, however, is the need to be realistic. It is unwise to tackle a boat that is too large for one's workspace or too far gone for one's available time, resources, and experience. Ultimately, whether their boats were smaller or larger, these authors undertook projects that offered an excellent chance of being completed rather than abandoned.

One way or another, people develop close relationships with wooden boats. Perhaps this is inevitable given the hands-on nature of wooden boat care. For some of this book's contributors, their boats represent the fulfillment of a lifelong dream. These owners demonstrate than one needn't have a large boat to derive endless hours of enjoyment. For more than one of the authors, the boats have literally become members of the family. One sometimes hears about boats or other heirlooms that are passed from one generation to another. Here we have actual examples! There's apparently little drive on the part of many wooden boat owners to "trade up" or use a boat as a fashion statement or as a high-decibel display of financial net worth. The joy provided by the boats in this book seems entirely unrelated to their size and that, in fact, may be this book's most valuable lesson.

— Stan Grayson
Marblehead, Massachusetts

1

Bringing Back a Rowboat

BY BURTON KNAPP, JR.

Semi-dories like the boat described in this chapter were popular as yacht tenders well into the first half of the 20th century. "Semi" refers to a key aspect of the boat's design. The forward portion of the hull resembled that of the round-sided Swampscott dories popular for racing on Boston's North Shore and elsewhere. But the aft sections were wider, had less rocker, and the transom was broader. All this improved the boat's stability and load carrying ability. It also made it possible for a later generation of boat owners to mount an outboard motor.

"The *Galloping Ghost* hasn't been in the water for three years," said my father-in-law. "Why don't you take her?" My wife, Nancy, was quick to accept the offer. Not only had Nancy literally grown up with the boat, but we both enjoyed rowing. With this seemingly innocent beginning, my adventure in repairing a wooden boat was launched!

The *Galloping Ghost* had been built in Bath, Maine in 1915 as a tender for Nancy's grandfather's motor yacht, a Dawn Cruiser that he kept in Marblehead, Massachusetts. She was named by Nancy's father after Red Grange, the elusive, three-time, All-American halfback — No.77 for the University of Illinois in the 1920s. After 20 years of service, the boat was stored in a corner of a barn on the family farm in western Massachusetts and almost forgotten. Years later in 1954, the boat was offered to Nancy's mother who shipped it to Martha's Vineyard, where the

family had a summer home. This became the boat's home as well, and for the next 44 years she was part of the family. Nancy's dad put on a 1 1/2-hp outboard, but soon replaced this with a 15-hp motor that propelled the *Ghost* and his young family on many a day's outing. Nancy's childhood memories include picnics and swims on the "outer beach", and curling up in the bow, out of the spray, as the boat pushed home against a stiff southwesterly breeze.

Given my wife's long history with the boat, the call of the *Galloping Ghost* was not to be denied. We went to the Vineyard to get the boat and trailered her back home to Maine. Anxious to go rowing, we immediately launched her at the town landing in Falmouth. I found that she leaked badly where one garboard plank had split, opening up a 1/4-inch gap. The gunwale was so tender that we could only ease her along with gentle strokes on

This photo, taken before the Galloping Ghost *was restored, shows the boat as she appeared for many years, running under outboard power off Edgartown, Massachusetts, with Nancy Knapp's parents aboard.*

the oars. But she floated, and she was ours!

That was in July of 1998. I was 51 and, as it happened, had a three-month sabbatical planned. Towards the end of my sabbatical, I would attend a two-week fundamentals course at the WoodenBoat School in Brooklin, Maine. I had long been interested in wooden boats and had always wanted to build one. With no experience in wooden boat repairs, I expected to scrape and repaint the *Ghost*, fix the few broken ribs, mend the gunwales, and have the boat complete before the WoodenBoat course began. That, at least, was the plan. Once started, however, it became apparent just how much work needed to be done to bring the *Ghost* back to life. Any desire to build a new wooden boat would have to wait.

A CONDITION REPORT

Year after year the *Galloping Ghost* had been dutifully painted, and the family always joked that it was the paint that held her together. I knew it was time to look beyond the paint and give the boat a thorough survey. I felt that a professional's opinion would be valuable and trailered the boat to a nearby yard where she was looked over by their "wooden boat man". An objective assessment of the boat now emerged.

The boat was 11' 3" long, and had a 49 1/2-inch beam. It was built as a lapstrake semi-dory — round sided and with a transom rather than the straight sides and tombstone stern of a classic Banks dory. As is typical of dory construction, she had a flat bottom made up of two pine boards running fore and aft, giving a maximum bottom width of 22 inches amidships. The boat was built of cedar planks laid over a mix of sawn white oak framing and steam-bent ribs. There were five strakes, or planks, on each side. All were in good condition except for the top edges of the sheer strakes and the garboard plank on one side. The gunwales were in poor repair, providing no support to the oarlocks, as we'd discovered on our initial sea trial.

A number of the ribs were broken or partially detached. The sawn oak frames — one at the forward thwart and one at the middle thwart — were likewise broken and had been reinforced. The thwarts were 1 1/8-inch pine, and the stern seat was gracefully fashioned of 1/2-inch pine. The transom was pine and had been reinforced to accept the pounding of the15-hp outboard motor. To a rowing enthusiast, this reinforced transom

The wobbly transom was among the more obvious areas that would need to be addressed during the boat's restoration.

was ugly and had to go!

Like so many small boats of her era, the *Ghost* had planking that was "iron fastened." The effective life span of the *Ghost's* galvanized nails had long ago run out, and there were ugly rust stains on the white hull from the deteriorating fastenings. Elsewhere in the boat, brass screws had been used to fasten pieces together.

The folks at the boatyard were supportive, and gave some useful, but fairly general, advice regarding what to do and how to do it. Mostly, I approached the project with commonsense and a copy of *Repairs*, by Walter J. Simmons. Later, of course, I would bring the knowledge and skills learned at the WoodenBoat School to the project.

THE WORK BEGINS

Because this was a small boat, I was able to keep her on the trailer. I was able to work outdoors in good weather and in the garage during inclement weather. The boat was light enough for me to turn over with my wife's help, supporting it on picnic table benches when working on the bottom and outside plank surfaces. After a week of superficial scraping and sanding, I was still operating under the illusion of being able to do a quick repair job in two months. Soon, however, it became apparent that to do a respectable restoration job, the boat would need to be completely stripped of all old paint and caulking. That decided, I removed the thwarts and stern seat, and I used a heat gun and putty knife to remove all paint. I worked outdoors or in an open garage with a fan set to carry fumes and paint dust (which I assumed could have lead) away from me. With the paint removed, it was easier to appraise the condition of the boat, and to locate the screws fastening the remainder of the interior joinery.

A hack saw blade made quick work of the old copper rivets holding the inwale in place. With my level of experience, I felt intimidated by the thought of replacing either the stem or the transom. I focused instead on the ribs and sawn frames, needing to decide which were sound, and could be left in place, and which needed replacement. The hack saw blade helped with deteriorating iron fastenings. I removed damaged ribs by splitting them lengthwise with a chisel at the intact fastenings.

An old chisel was used to remove fairing compound and caulk from over countersunk screw heads. The screws were brass, and their removal allowed removal of the breast hook, quarter knees, and floors. The keelson on the exterior (which covers the center seam where the two floor boards come together) seemed intact and was left in place. A similar piece had been fitted on the inside. It was in sections between the floors, and embedded in caulk or a bedding compound. It seemed like a late addition to help limit leaking along the seam. I thought it possibly harmful — a moisture trap — and removed the sections with no intention of replacing them.

Fortunately the boat retained its shape despite removal of some of the ribs, frames, and all of the interior joinery and inwale. There is a tendency for a boat to splay wider when the thwarts, which provide structural strength to the hull, are removed. I was careful to note that the beam measurement from sheer to sheer didn't change. It was fixed at the original width when the new thwarts were installed.

With the boat turned upside down, I needed to address the deteriorating iron fastenings along the laps. These were certainly a cosmetic problem, causing rust stains on the paint, but I feared they presented a structural problem as well. In fact, two laps had opened up and needed refastening. Would the entire boat need refastening to make it sound? One opinion from the local boat yard was to refasten the boat by cutting out each old fastening with a hole saw, plugging the hole with a cedar plug and

epoxy, and then refastening with new copper rivets. This was more than I had bargained for. Besides, most of the laps seemed secure despite the rust stains.

I arrived at a method of repair which seemed to work: I ground away the exterior, rusted end of the iron fastenings along with the adjacent iron-poisoned wood. I used a cordless drill fitted with a one-inch diameter grinding bit. I then filled the resulting cavity with epoxy filler. This sealed off the iron, and has thus far prevented further deterioration of the iron fastening and further discoloration from rust.

REBUILDING

The gap between the starboard garboard plank and bottom plank, where the *Galloping Ghost* had leaked so badly, seemed like the place to start rebuilding. The gap was clean and 1/4-inch wide by about 14 inches long. It was easy to plane a scrap of cedar planking to size and epoxy it into position. The battered edges of the sheer planks came next. Following Walt Simmons's succinct instructions and clear illustrations, I cut away sections of the damaged planks, and I graved (inset) pieces from new cedar plank stock by fitting and epoxying them into place.

The trick to fitting a new section of plank along the edge of the sheer was to cut the new section in the shape of a trapezoid, and wider than needed. If the fit is perfect, the extra width is

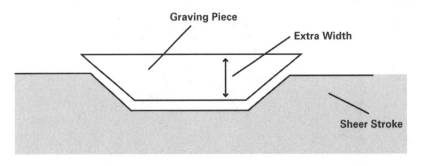

New cedar graving pieces were used to repair the Galloping Ghost's *battered sheer strakes.*

simply planed flush with the sheer once the piece is glued in place. If you cut the new section too short, you can plane from the bottom, allowing the piece to settle into place while still retaining enough width to bring it flush with the sheer.

Still not wanting to address the stem and transom, I turned next to refastening the laps which had opened up. The iron fastenings had failed completely along two of the lap joints, in a two to three foot area. I gently cleaned the lap bevel of any old paint, caulk, and irregularities. I applied 5200 marine adhesive to the lap joint where it was open, and drew the planks together with several well placed drywall screws. I used a large washer to prevent damage to the exterior face of the plank as the screw was tightened. On the interior, I drove the screw through the lap and into a block of scrap wood. Tightening the screw

pulled the lap together, sandwiched between the washer and the wood block, without damage to the soft cedar. With the lap drawn together, I placed copper rivets every two to three inches along the lap. Then, I removed the drywall screws and replaced them with a few final rivets. The 5200 Marine Adhesive made for a watertight joint and added strength as well (Having sealed the old iron fastenings in epoxy, I didn't worry about using two dissimilar metals — iron and copper — on the boat.)

While anxious to try steam bending new ribs, I first replaced the bottom cleats, or floors, the stout oak pieces that run across the fore-and-aft bottom planks that are a typical feature of dory construction. The bottom cleats serve to fasten the bottom planks together. I used the old cleats as patterns for the new ones. Each cleat was

An 11-foot boat can start to look pretty big when one comes face to face with the full extent of the work it needs. Here, several of the cleats joining the bottom boards have been removed for replacement and some of the broken, steam-bent ribs have been removed.

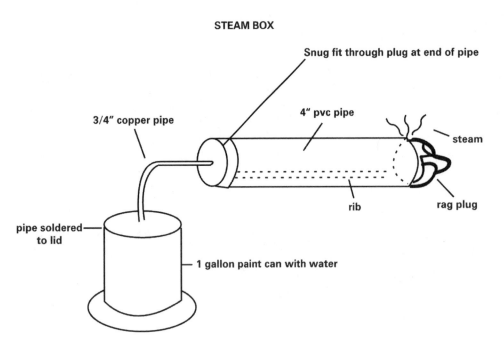

STEAM BOX

Snug fit through plug at end of pipe

3/4" copper pipe

4" pvc pipe

steam

rib

rag plug

pipe soldered to lid

1 gallon paint can with water

Creating a "steam box" is often a matter of ingenuity. This simple setup, borrowed by the author from a friend, was able to hold the new 30" long oak ribs that were key components in the restoration project.

primed with Interlux White Undercoater, as was the inside of the boat. When the primer had dried, I set the cleats in bedding compound and fastened them with new brass screws through the existing screw holes in the bottom. I applied a little wax to the threads of the screws. This made it easier to drive the screws into the snug, predrilled pilot holes in the oak floors. I used butcher's wax because it was on the shelf in the shop. Beeswax or bar soap work well also.

Time to steam ribs! I borrowed a steam box from a friend. The box was a four-inch diameter PVC pipe, long enough to accept the 30" x 3/4" x 3/8" white oak which I had worked up for the ribs. One end of the pipe was fitted with an end cover that had 3/4-inch copper pipe fitted to it. The pipe was soldered to the lid on a one-gallon metal paint can. When water in the can was brought to a boil on the kitchen stove, steam filled the PVC pipe which was positioned horizontally, its open end plugged by a cloth.

This steam box worked well, but the oak was

dry and could not be easily bent despite adequate steam time. The solution was to soak the rib stock in water for a week. This made it much more pliable when steamed, more like green wood which is ideal for steaming. Dry or green, straight-grained stock is essential. The steamed ribs were pressed into position and held with a couple of drywall screws. Once cool, the screws were removed, the ribs allowed to dry, and their edges smoothed. I applied a primer before repositioning and riveting them into place (with rivets at the laps). I avoided placing a rivet mid-plank so as not to split a plank.

During all this work, I had taken care to preserve the somewhat fragile stem. In turning the boat over for the floors, however, the stem caught, and the top six inches broke off, splitting along the grain. I fashioned a new top piece out

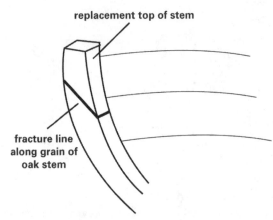

replacement top of stem

fracture line along grain of oak stem

A piece of white oak was used to fashion a new upper portion of the boat's stem when the old one broke. The new piece was attached with epoxy.

of white oak, and epoxied it into place. The real strength at the bow, however, came from the new breast hook. It was made of 1 5/8-inch white oak. It solidly reinforced the still fragile sheer strakes with their graving pieces and the mended stem. I made the breast hook in three pieces, following an excellent description in Walter Simmons's book.

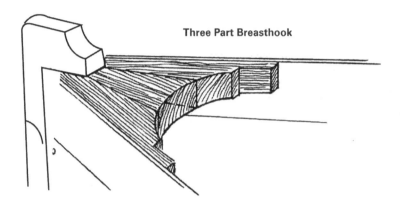

Three Part Breasthook

A stout 1 5/8" white oak breast hook is the component that does most to reinforce the boat's bow.

hull two inches from the outboard face of the old transom and cut along the line with a handsaw. Cutting into the old boat was disquieting, but it was remarkable how easy it was to saw a boat in two! When I was done, I had shortened the boat by two inches but left clean plank ends to refasten to the new transom. Removing the old transom by unfastening it at the plank ends would have preserved boat length, but left me with worn and battered plank ends to refasten.

Cutting off the old transom had been nerve-wracking, but the most difficult part of this aft-end project was now to come. This involved cutting the new 3/4-inch mahogany transom to size, and then developing the right bevels to allow a snug fit against the insides of the planks. I used a cardboard template, scribing it to the inside surface of the planks, 3/4 inches from the plank ends. I transferred the pattern to the mahogany, and cut the new

Unable to avoid it any longer, I now needed to address the issue of the transom. Replacing the battered, painted pine transom was a must. I dreamed of a bright-finished mahogany transom. Finding good advice again in Walter Simmons's book, I gained the courage to tackle the job. I literally cut the old transom off by sawing through the strakes. Before starting, I placed a Spanish windlass around the stern to prevent the sides of the boat from splaying out once freed from the old transom.

I drew a line around the

A Spanish windlass was used to hold the boat's stern in shape when it was finally time to remove the old transom. The author used a handsaw to do the job, which shortened the Galloping Ghost *by two inches but left clean, solid plank ends to fasten to the new transom.*

transom on the band saw without any bevels.

The outside edge of the transom needed to be prepared so that the planks would fit snugly against it. The bevel on the transom's bottom edge was uniform, straight across, and easy to pick off with the bevel square, but all the other areas required more meticulous bevel work. Since the planks curved in at the stern, the outboard dimensions of the transom were slightly less than the inboard dimensions and the transom was beveled accordingly. Once the transom was installed, the plank ends protruded a bit past the outboard surface of the transom, and were easily planed flush with a block plane.

Although the fit of the planks against the transom was about 95 percent perfect, it wasn't 100 percent. This resulted from my having applied the measured bevel at each plank to the transom, marking the knuckle, the angle where the planks came together at each lap on the inboard surface of the transom, but not taking into account the exact knuckle location at the outboard transom surface. However, I found that 5200 compound applied between the transom and the planks made for a "perfect" fit, and the transom was securely fastened in place with brass screws, two at each plank. These were countersunk at the plank surface, and the pilot hole very carefully aligned with the center of the transom's edge and with the angle of the transom. This was quite difficult given the thinness of the transom. I misplaced one screw and it buckled the inboard surface of the transom as I drove it home. Fortunately it was below the level of the sternsheets, and out of sight. I used wax again on the screws before driving them into the hard wood. Extra wood was left at the top of the transom so that I could give the top edge a pleasing curve once the transom was in place, and also to allow for an error in fitting the transom. The concept is similar to that described in fitting a graving piece.

With the transom in place, I could build the

Progress! The boat's new 3/4" mahogany transom has been installed, secured by two screws through each plank. Also visible here are the boat's new ribs, the oak thwarts with their mahogany risers, the breast hook and repaired stem.

remaining interior joinery. Thwart risers were made by resawing a 1 3/4" x 3/4" piece of mahogany to make fairly flexible strips of wood. They bent easily to the curve of the boat and were fastened to the ribs with small brass screws. They were set so that the final height of the thwarts was the same as the original height. The thwarts were fashioned from 3/4-inch white oak. In retrospect, pine would have worked as well and would have saved weight. The thwarts rested on the risers, and with the thwart knees riveted to the inwales they provided structural strength to the boat.

The thwart knees were made from one-inch white oak. Because the oak was straight-grained, and I wanted the grain to run with the narrow upper arm that would be riveted to the sheer strake and to the inwale, I left extra width in the lower leg of the knee. This was intended to compensate for the weakness caused by the cross grain. In fact, one knee did split along the grain and needed a brass screw and epoxy to restore its integrity. It would have been better to use steam-bent wood or wood from a natural tree crook or knee.

I did use wood from a tamarack knee for the quarter knees and transom knee. A template of each knee was laid out on 1 1/4" slabs of tamarack so as to take advantage of the natural curve in the wood's grain. The slabs of tamarack were cut on a commercial-sized band saw at a local boat shop, the knees cut out on my home 10" band saw, and final adjustments to the bevels made with a block plane. Each knee was fastened in place with screws, using epoxy for a strong joint.

Fitting the inwales — 1 1/2" x 5/8" oak — was the next challenge. It required careful attention to detail. Each inwale needed to follow a fair curve and fit flush against the inboard end of each rib and thwart knee. They also had to fit into notches in the breast hook at the bow and notches in the quarter knees at the stern. Because some of the old ribs were quite worn and their ends were thinner than the ends of the new ribs, I cut away old wood and spliced in new wood with epoxy to build thickness. At the same time, some of the ends of the new ribs needed to be reduced in thickness with a rasp. The trick to cutting the inwale to the exact length so as to fit snugly in the breast hook and quarter knee notches is described in detail by Walter Simmons. I followed his instructions closely.

Starting at the breast hook, the inwale was bent into position and held with clamps. Drawing the inwale snug against each rib caused the inwale to pull away from the notch at the breast hook. Before pro-

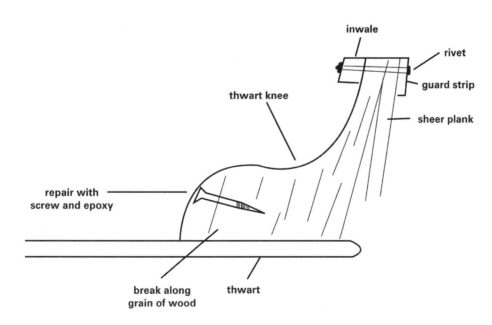

Inch-thick white oak was used for the semi-dory's thwart knees. When one knee split across the grain, it was repaired with epoxy and a screw.

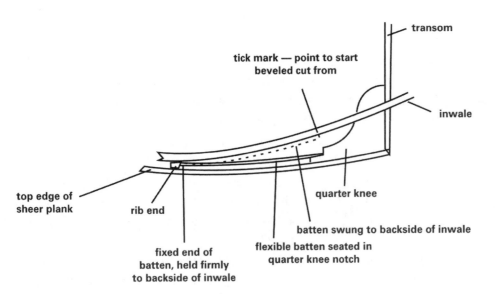

Installing the inwales was a tricky task. The author used a two-foot-long flexible batten to help determine the inwale's precise length for a snug fit into the tamarack quarter knee.

ceeding past midship, the aft end of the inwale was given a firm tap with a hammer. This drove the inwale forward, snug into the notch at the breast hook. If the fit in the notch is not perfect, one or more passes through the joint with a thin hacksaw blade can correct it.

More clamps were placed working aft until within two feet of the quarter knee. I left extra length at the aft end of the inwale so that I could tick off the final length accurately. To do this, a thin flexible wooden batten, about two feet in length, was laid against the outboard side of the inwale with the end of the batten placed snugly in the quarter knee notch. Without moving the forward end of the batten, I swung the aft end from the notch to the inwale, I ticked off the intersection at the top outboard corner of the inwale. This was the starting point for making the beveled cut of the inwale. A cut with the proper bevel was made, and the inwale swung snugly into the notch in the quarter knee. The inwale was now snug against each rib end, thwart knee, quarter knee, and breast hook. It was held in place with clamps.

I cut a guard strip (or outwale) measuring 1 1/8" x 7/16" from white oak stock and placed it opposite the inwale against the upper outer edge of the sheer strake. Fastening was done with rivets, each of which passed through the guard strip, the upper edge of the sheer strake, a rib end, and finally the inwale. Rivets were placed similarly at the thwart knees, quarter knees, and breast hook. This made for a very solid gunwale. It tied the thwarts to the sheer strakes, thereby adding overall stiffness to the boat's structure.

In replacing the stern seat, I copied the style of the old seat using 1/2-inch white pine, but left spaces between the boards to prevent moisture from being trapped. The seat was supported by a narrow board fixed to the transom and a forward support resting on a rib both port and starboard.

When it came time to fashion a new skeg, I eyeballed the dimensions and cut the skeg from inch-thick oak stock. The skeg was fastened to the keelson with countersunk brass screws. What looked right, however, didn't work in practice. The skeg was not deep enough to allow the boat to track and I ended up adding another inch to its depth. To do this, I simply added a new piece to the existing skeg and screwed and epoxied it into place. The deeper skeg allowed better tracking without diminishing the boat's responsive handling.

FINISHING

I had primed the interior of the boat with Interlux before installing the floors and ribs. The center seam between the two bottom boards was caulked with 5200 compound. When the 5200 dried, I finished the inside with two coats of Interlux Blue Gray.

I knew that the exterior of the cedar planking would need attention after decades of bumps, refinishing, and exposure. I used a West System epoxy fairing compound to smooth surface defects. I applied the fairing compound much like you'd apply "mud" or spackling compound to dry-wall — with a four-inch-wide putty knife. After hardening, it was sanded to a smooth finish. The key was the consistency of the compound. The work was tedious, but because the boat is old I did not strive for a mirror smooth finish. I accepted a pleasing, used look.

Since most of the laps were not refastened, I was concerned about their being water-tight. Again, turning to Walter Simmons, I used a technique he describes of running a bead of caulk along each exterior lap. (I used an old paint scraper to make a v-shaped gouge along each lap so that the edge of the lap joint would more readily accept a bead of caulk. 5200 Compound was applied, and smoothed with a finger.) Having the boat caulked like this allows it to be stored on land, and yet be watertight at each launching. Without caulk, most joints in a wooden boat leak until the wood swells after being in the water for several days. The exterior finish consisted of two coats of Interlux primer followed by three coats of

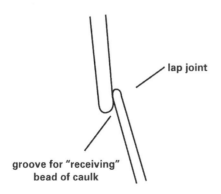

A bead of 5200 caulk was used to fill a v-shaped groove along each of the boat's lapped planks to resist leaks.

Interlux Malachy Green.

I chose to use Cetol rather than varnish for the brightwork because it's easy to apply, and no sanding is needed or recommended between coats, although a light buffing with a nylon scuff pad can be done. I applied two coats of Cetol Marine followed by three coats of Cetol Marine Gloss. The Cetol Marine, which I used as a primer but many use as the only coating, is tinted, giving the pine, oak, and tamarack a pleasing yellow-orange hue. There was no effect on the darker mahogany. As this is written Cetol has introduced a new product called Marine Light. It has no tint, which some might find desirable.

I waited until the hull painting was complete before fastening the guard strip and inwale, both of which had been finished with Cetol Marine and Cetol Marine Gloss. The oar lock pads, which were made of mahogany, were bright finished before fastening them securely to the inwale and guardrail with copper rivets. It was satisfying to apply a little artistry in their shaping on the band saw.

IN THE WATER
By summer's end 2000, more than 24 months after I had begun work, the *Galloping Ghost* had been restored. Because of my unheated garage and Maine winters, I worked on the boat for only six months out of the year. The work was done in my spare time. The restoration was a time-consuming labor of love, but it was great fun! What's more I had managed to do the job with only average woodworking skills and no prior experience in boat building. Attending the WoodenBoat School fundamentals course was most helpful. It gave me familiarity with the materials, the tools, and the techniques which I put to good use. Most helpful was instruction in sharpening tools, steam-bending oak ribs, riveting with copper nails and roves, and actually shaping and installing a quarter knee and inwale.

The *Galloping Ghost* has been a pleasure to

The end result — careful workmanship, and the contrast of a dark green hull and brightly varnished trim yield a beautiful boat.

row, and she never fails to elicit compliments. I usually trailer her to the town landing and take her for a row when I have a free afternoon. She rows best with one person, however, she easily carries two passengers and gear as befits her original intent for use as a tender. The boat is too small to allow both rowing stations to be used at the same time. The front rowing station is best used to balance the boat when there is only one passenger — rower in the bow, passenger in the stern. I use 8 1/2- foot oars. (My wife and I have since purchased a 14' Piscataqua Wherry, which we row as a couple. It is a lovely fiberglass boat with two fixed-seat rowing stations. It is produced locally by Bay of Maine Boats. We use nine-foot Shaw & Tenney oars. We find it large enough and fast enough to take day trips to the islands along the coast here in Maine.)

Using 20/20 hindsight, I now see that I made

a mistake in not refastening the planks at the stem. Initially the *Galloping Ghost* didn't leak a drop, but alas, it does now along the stem and along the garboard planks where they join the bottom at the bow. Perhaps it is time to replace the floorboards, which for so many years had kept feet and gear dry aboard the *Galloping Ghost*. Back to the workshop!

BOAT SPECS

Designer	Unknown
Type	Semi-Dory
Year Built	1915
Length x Beam	11'3" x 4' 1 1/2"
Construction	Cedar planks over oak frames, mahogany transom, oak and tamarack knees

TOOLS

Initially, my tools were simple: a hack saw blade for cutting through old fastenings, a putty knife, a paint scraper, and a heat gun for removing layers of old paint and caulk. Before the project was completed, however, the full list of useful tools included:

- Band saw
- Radial arm saw
- Block plane
- #12 smoothing plane
- Chisels
- Cordless drill
- Brace and screw driver bit
- Miter square
- Clamps
- Ball peen hammer
- Backing iron
- Nippers
- Steam box

A friend lent his help with a planer, joiner, and table saw. We used these to join two pieces of mahogany with a spline and epoxy to create the transom. The most useful handsaw I used was a Japanese saw that cuts on the pull stroke.

MATERIALS

- West System Epoxy
- 5200 Marine Adhesive Sealant by 3M
- Cetol Marine and Cetol Marine Gloss for bright work
- Interlux White Undercoater 279 and Interlux Premium Yacht Enamel: Malachy Green #341 and Blue Gray #282
- Copper nails and roves, brass screws
- Bedding compound
- Sand paper and sponge block
- Drywall screws

About the Author: Burton Knapp, Jr. was born in 1947 and raised in New Jersey, where his family spent summers at the Jersey shore. He learned to sail on a Sunfish in Cape Cod Bay. According to Burt, "The world started to change for me when my friend and I gave up the rowboat for a speedboat, and catching frogs for water skiing and thinking about girls. I've come full circle. Now, as an adult, I'm back to messing around again in rowboats."

Today Burt Knapp practices Family Medicine in Maine. He and his wife enjoy the Maine coast where they brought up their three children, summering on the islands, rowing dinghies, and sailing a Rhodes 19. Burt is also on the board of the Compass Project in Portland, Maine, a not-for-profit group helping introduce area junior high and high school students to the discipline and fun of boat building and rowing. With WoodenBoat, the Compass Project sponsored Portland's first annual Family Boat Building event in July 2004.

2

A Chris-Craft Utility

BY RUSS BALLENGER

America's post-war boating boom was already underway when the 18-footer that is the subject of this chapter was built in 1952. Even as fiberglass and aluminum boat companies began making their first serious inroads, Chris-Craft stuck firmly to its traditional ways, and initially saw little threat from boats made of anything but wood. The company's Utility models were first introduced during the Depression in the early '30s. These all-purpose boats, somewhat plain and less expensive by comparison to the firm's runabouts, found an ongoing market and evolved as the years passed. With its open interior, the utility type — "Sportsman" was Chris-Craft's official name for this model — was useful for a wide variety of recreational activities. Finished in gleaming varnish, boats like these remain as hard to resist today as they were when new. Restoring a boat like this raises immediate questions about how close to original one wishes to adhere. That question is for the individual to decide and thus, within limits, probably has no right or wrong answer.

As a baby boomer who grew up in the '60s, I have memories of sit-ins, muscle cars, and camping trips to northern Wisconsin lakes. There it was quite common to see and hear a wide variety of glistening wooden boats, and I quickly became hooked on the dream of some day owning one. As things developed, it took some 25 years for that dream to be realized but it finally happened in the fall of 1992. That's when I spotted a *Milwaukee Journal* ad for a 1952 Chris-Craft Sportsman with a six-cylinder, 95-hp engine. While this boat wasn't exactly the 1939 double cockpit, barrel-back Chris-Craft cus-

tom runabout that I once had envisioned, it struck me that here was just the boat for a fellow with a wife, three kids, and a house that was an ongoing project in itself.

When I called the owner, I found a gentleman in circumstances somewhat similar to my own. He'd recently started a major renovation to his home and felt he would not have time to devote to the project. Three hours later, I was standing in front of Chris-Craft hull number U-18-1073. The boat, in the beginning stages of restoration, was sitting on a reasonably sound-looking trailer. My first impression was a bit disappointing. The boat's hardware had been stripped and except for the newly painted blue bottom, the hull and deck were various shades of natural mahogany depending on how much sanding had been done.

Closer examination, however, showed that the wood on the boat was sound with no visible signs of rot. While much of the hardware was in boxes, the majority of it was in fact there, and it was in more or less usable condition. The motor, while appearing to be intact, showed signs of having been exposed to the weather, and I was unable to move it by cranking on the flywheel. Given my limited knowledge of what I was getting into, this old Chris-Craft looked to me to be a good candidate for restoration.

The boat's owner had done some research about it. From the Mariner's Museum Library in Newport News, Virginia he'd obtained a copy of the original Chris-Craft Boat Equipment Record checklist dated October 21, 1952 and indicating the boat's original destination had been Norton Brothers at Green Lake, Wisconsin. He also had copies of a sales brochure for that year and a price list. The base price of this boat had been $3,047.00, a significant sum in 1952. After some discussion with the owner and reflection on what I might be getting myself into, I made an offer and it was accepted. I had no way of knowing it, but I

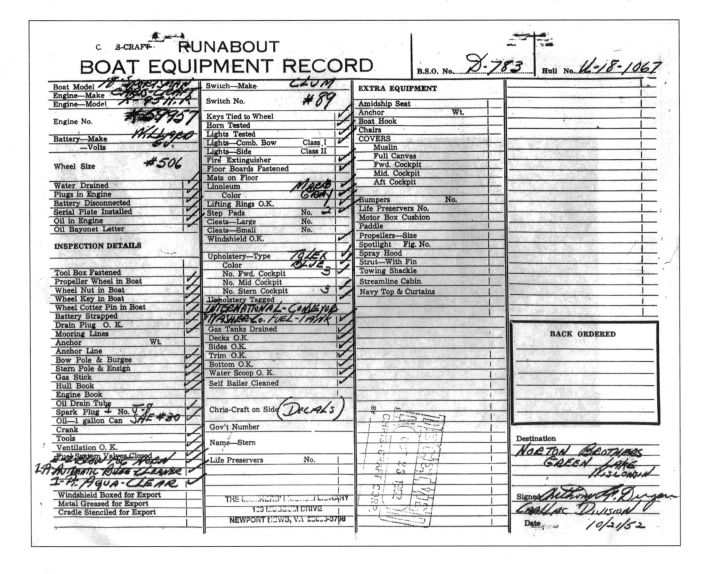

had just begun a project that would not be completed until 11 years had passed.

When I took on the challenge of restoring what would later be named *Vintage Vixen,* perhaps the single most important decision I faced was deciding how close I'd keep to original manufacturer specifications. Using techniques and materials similar to Chris-Craft's in 1952 would result in an historically correct boat. Such a boat would garner a lot of points at boat shows using The Antique And Classic Boat Society's judging system. (The judging system is available online and is worth reading to get an understanding of what details are considered and how they're weighted.)

A lot has changed since 1952, of course. To cite just a few considerations: it was necessary to decide if vinyl-covered wires should replace original cloth, if the electrical system should be updated to 12-volt from six-volt, if carpeted decks should replace linoleum, and so forth. In the end I based my decisions on the fact that the boat was intended for everyday use; it needed to be practical, not a showpiece. Thus, although I wanted to keep the boat as original as possible, there would need to be changes from Chris-Craft's original methods and materials.

Ultimately, the most dramatic departure from original would involve the boat's bottom. While I live on the Wisconsin River, I did not intend to leave the boat in the water. Instead, the boat would sit on the trailer in the garage until I'd use it, and would return there when done. For this reason I wanted a watertight boat not requiring soaking to swell bottom planks. There are many ways to accomplish this goal but I settled on glass and epoxy finish over the original planking. I also decided early on that the upholstery and flooring would be upgraded to a more comfortable and visually pleasing level.

As with any project, one must determine the work needing to be done, select the materials and equipment to complete the work, and then chart

a course. Although I'd performed a superficial survey of the Sportsman when I bought the boat, I did a much more thorough inspection after I brought her home. The results were:

Hull: the overall condition of the hull was good with no evidence of rot. However, there were several areas showing wear and abuse that would require attention. For example, on the front starboard side, a plank was cracked and dented, likely from bouncing off a pier. The plank would need replacing. The tops of the gunwales were worn and dented from countless passengers getting on and off. The top two boards of the transom were split and moving away from each other. The front seat framework was badly worn. The bottom had been stripped and painted blue, possibly its original color. Now it would need to be stripped again. Many bungs were loose and would require replacement. The caulk in the front deck was cracked and would need to be removed and replaced.

Hardware: I made a list of each piece of hardware and its condition. While the chrome could use replating on many pieces, most were presentable enough and could be refinished at a later date after the boat was back in the water. There were also a few missing pieces, such as rear deck vents, gas cap, windshields, and front and rear masts. A previous owner had cut a slot in the cutwater and installed a hook to aid in getting the boat on the trailer. The slot would have to be filled to return the stem to its original configuration.

Motor and mechanicals: Not being much of an engine mechanic, I intended to have a complete overhaul of the components done by a professional. To my eye, the motor and running gear appeared to be complete and in fair condition.

Trailer: The boat came with a dual-axle trailer of unknown age or weight classification. It

The boat came with a trailer that had been sand blasted and painted, and the author installed new tires and wiring. The damaged plank seen here was among those that required replacing.

appeared to be a bit on the light side for the weight presently sitting on it. Since my intent was not to be making long trips when the project was complete, I decided to rewire the trailer and install new tires. The seller had sand blasted and painted the trailer; the only other change I eventually made was to lengthen the winch support in order to use the front lifting hook on the boat to pull it onto the trailer.

In beginning the project I had no experience in wooden boat construction or maintenance. I had experience with home construction and remodeling, having owned a home for the previous 10 years, and having done much of the work to update and add to our 1960s river home. During that period, I had replaced my original workshop in the basement backroom with a new 24' x 48' shop for several reasons: I was constantly making a mess in the house, the kids were getting older,

another bedroom was needed, and projects were getting bigger and more elaborate. Half of the new structure was workshop and the other half garage space. Both sides were insulated and, when needed, heated with a wood-burning furnace that was eventually converted to a fuel oil system.

My shop was equipped with the usual woodworking equipment necessary for home remodeling. This included: 10-inch table saw, floor standing drill press, various corded and cordless drills, hand sanders, belt sander, router and router table, jig saws, 12-inch compound miter saw, airless sprayer, 4" x 36" belt and six-inch disk sander, circular saws, as well as the usual hand tools. During the course of the project I purchased a 12-inch Delta thickness planer, and a Ryobi detail sander for sanding in tight spaces. I also installed a shop vacuum system to control dust, a major problem when trying to obtain a good contaminate-free finish. The few other pieces I didn't have were borrowed from friends and family, including such things as come-alongs for rolling the hull over, a laser used to reestablish the water line, and a wood moisture meter.

Stripping and Cleaning

As the boat's restoration had already been started by the previous owner, much of the hardware had been removed, saving me that chore. Additionally, the rough sanding to remove the finish had been completed and a new rear deck had been installed. A new engine cover had also been constructed. The previous owner intended to do his restoration with the motor, steering, fuel, cooling and electrical systems still in place. However, knowing the engine would be rebuilt as part of the restoration, I decided to remove it and all of the remaining mechanical systems and hardware. As the various pieces of the remaining systems were disassembled and removed, they were put into large zip lock bags. The bags were labeled with information on their function, location, assembly instructions and, when necessary, a drawing. I used a notebook to record the same information for larger pieces and for the interaction of all smaller assemblies. This technique worked for me because I didn't have a digital camera or camcorder to record a visual reference to aid in assembly. As events developed, reassembly would not take place until years later.

Thanks to my employer, my dad and I were able to use a forklift from work to remove the engine. After stripping off the starter, generator, carburetor and fuel pump, we wrapped a chain around a fork on the lift and hooked it to the lifting hook on the engine. Then, we removed the bolts from the engine mounts and lifted the engine from the hull. The hull's interior side planking was removed with some difficulty as the sanding of the planking, performed by the previous owner to remove the old finish, also removed some of the slots of the exposed Phillips screws.

I used a knife to clean varnish from remaining screw heads and, in many cases, the tip of the knife was enough to turn the screws out. In other cases a tap from a hammer on the screwdriver handle to set the blade in the slots did the trick. In some extreme cases, the head had to be drilled off and the shaft of the screw extracted with vise grips after the plank had been popped off.

The backs of each board were numbered and a drawing of the location made. Next, we removed the front seat assemblies and dash and set them aside for later rebuilding and refinishing. With the removal of the floorboards, the boat was basically stripped to the bare hull with front and rear deck. During removal of the interior planking, a distinctive line of silt and sand was found two-thirds of the way up on the inside of the hull. From this, we surmised that the boat had once sat on the bottom in about three feet of water. To clean the hull of silt, sand, and 40 years of dirt, we used a solution of TSP applied with stiff scrub brushes. After thorough scrubbing and rinsing, we discovered that the interior wood and original red bilge paint were in surprisingly good shape.

Planking Repairs and Replacement

It was now time to address the structural items noted in my survey: the plank on the front starboard side, the top two transom boards, the gunwale tops, and the front seat framing. Not needing a lot of new mahogany for these areas, I contacted a boat restoration shop located about two hours away and purchased four 16-foot planks of varying widths. Since the planks on the hull needing replacement were all approximately 1/2-inch thick, and the planks that I had purchased were 1 1/4-inch thick, I took two of them to a local millworker. There, a band saw cut the planks in half giving me four 9/16-inch thick boards, 1/8-inch lost to the saw blade. Two planks provided the stock for new gunwales, while one was used to replace the plank on the starboard front side. I would use the last one on the transom. I eventu-

Here, the damaged starboard plank has been removed. A new plank, made of 9/16" thick mahogany, was installed. Later, the top two transom planks were also replaced as were damaged areas atop the gunwales.

ally used one of the remaining full thickness planks to rebuild seat frames. A planer brought the new planks to the proper thickness.

The top two transom planks, each approximately seven inches wide, were removed without much difficulty. The glue used to hold the bungs in place had dried out over the previous 40 years and was extremely brittle. I removed the majority of the bungs by tapping a flat-bladed screwdriver onto a bung and then twisting the blade. A knife and awl removed the final bits. This same technique was also used to replace the loose, stained, and damaged plugs on the rest of the hull.

Once the transom's fasteners were removed, a tap from a rubber mallet on the backside of each transom board sufficed to free the planking. Since the old planks removed from the transom and the hull were in good shape, we used them to make an exact copy in the new wood. I clamped the old planks onto the prepared stock and used

a router with a Formica countertop trimming bit. The bit was set so the ball bearing roller (on the end of the bit) rolled on the edge of the original wood. The cutting blades exactly reproduced the shape in the new plank. I used the same technique later for the gunwale tops.

The seat frames, which had rounded corners, dents, and cracks from countless passengers moving about the cockpit, were intact enough to get good dimensions for the new construction. Once again, I clamped old parts to new stock and used the router to reproduce the replacement pieces.

Bottom Work

After stripping the boat, all accessible fasteners were tightened. The hull was now ready to be rolled over. With the assistance of my dad, we slid the hull off the trailer onto old mattresses on the floor of the garage. Two 4 x 4s were then secured

Old mattresses provided the cushioning needed when it was time roll over the hull to begin work on the bottom.

Come-alongs securely anchored to the garage wall were key to rolling over the hull safely and without damage.

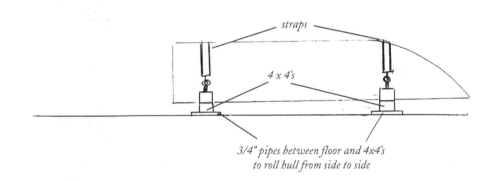

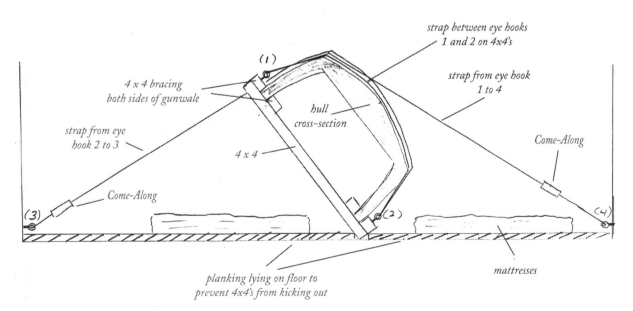

The diagrams should help others facing the problem of turning over a hull within the workspace. Once the hull was inverted, the mattresses were removed and 3/4" pipes placed beneath it. This permitted the boat to be shifted as necessary within the garage.

across the top of the cockpit with blocking attached on both sides of the gunwales. The 4 x 4s were held in place with straps around the bottom. They were intended to both retain the hull shape and protect the gunwales during the roll. I installed hooks in the 4 x 4s and attached these to come-alongs, anchored in the base of the garage walls. This permitted us to pull the hull over and gently lower it down. The come-alongs needed a little assistance in the form of my muscle power — lifting and lowering at the point between the two 4 x 4s — but, overall, it went smoothly. The same method was used to roll the hull back over after completing the bottom work. Once the hull was upside down and off the mattresses, 3/4-inch pipes were placed under and perpendicular to the 4 x 4s. This enabled us to roll the hull from side to side in the garage.

With the boat upside down, the nicely painted bottom was accessible. As I intended to epoxy and glass the bottom, all that nice paint had to go. I did not want to further thin the bottom with sanding, so I decided to use paint stripper instead. Because the paint was fresh, the stripping was easy. I used a putty knife and steel wool as necessary to assist in the process.

The inverted hull gave rather comfortable access to the boat's sides. Since removal of the finish and rough sanding had been completed by the previous owner, my first sanding was performed with 100-grit sand paper. I made two additional passes using 150- and then 220-grit paper. All of the sanding was done by hand in the direction of the grain using a sanding block rather than an electric sander. While this proved to be more work, I felt it gave better results.

Next, I replaced bungs as necessary and made preparations for staining. There have been many articles written about proper methods of making and installing bungs. Here's what I

A borrowed laser was used to draw a straight, new water line, which was marked in pencil.

learned as I moved ahead: use wood of similar age and grain pattern when cutting new bungs. I saved old planking, framing, and scraps for this purpose. I used a four-flute plug cutter to produce new bungs. When it was necessary to drill holes for fasteners prior to plugging, I selected a drill bit that was properly sized to the screw. Each hole was countersunk using an adjustable depth gauge. I decided to use glue that would be water resistant and would dry hard and brittle. I used Elmer's Carpenter's Wood Glue (Weather-Tite). I inserted the bungs in the holes, aligning the grain with the plank. I trimmed excess with a chisel and then sanded each bung level with the plank's surface. The time spent properly installing bungs would later show in the finished product.

With the hull prepared for finishing, it was time to mark the water line. A laser, on loan from work, was attached to a tripod and aligned using remnants of the original water line which I had found when removing the bottom paint. Once the laser was aligned, its beam was projected down the boat's side and I made pencil marks to produce a new, straight line. In order to protect the recently sanded sides of the hull from the work that was about to be performed on the bottom below the water line, I used masking tape and plastic. Then, the mahogany bottom was lightly sanded in preparation for the first coat of epoxy.

As I looked ahead to fiberglassing the bottom, I planned to work safely. Throughout this stage of the project I wore gloves, shop coat, respirator, and eye protection. This was especially important since I was working in a confined space with minimal ventilation. I used foam-covered rollers and brushes to work the two-part mixture into the surface and into all the joints between the planks. A scotch pad and water were used between each coat to remove the blush that occurs during the epoxy hardening process. This prepared the surface for the next epoxy coat — epoxy mixed with microfibers to form a paste applied with wide plastic spatulas. This paste acted as filler for the joints between the planks and any imperfections on the surface.

I used 60-inch wide, six-ounce, glass mat on the boat's bottom. I then applied the preparatory coat of epoxy from back to front, I laid the matting from side to side, overlapping each edge by several inches. Additional coats of epoxy were applied to fill the matting until a smooth surface was obtained. A common source of leakage on hulls like mine is the point where the prop shaft passes through the hull. In the July/August 1988 *Classic Boating* magazine article entitled "To Glass or Not to Glass, That is the Question" by James Lee, I found a technique to remedy this problem — a fiberglass tube that, when filled with grease, would seal the shaft. I wrapped wax paper around the prop shaft to act as a bond breaker. Glass mat was then wrapped around the wax paper twice. I used epoxy to fill the mat. I repeated this three times, producing a tube consisting of six layers of mat filled with epoxy. The new tube was slid off the shaft and wax paper. I then installed the strut on the hull and slid the shaft into position.

We now slid a temporary alignment block with a "V" cut into position under the shaft about four inches from where it entered the hull. The block's location was carefully marked on the hull since this would be the guide to align the shaft during installation of my newly made shaft tube. I removed the shaft and enlarged the shaft hole to allow the tube to penetrate with just a little room for positioning. A coat of epoxy was applied to the inside of the hole to prepare the surface. Finally, the shaft was slid into the tube and both were slid into the hull and strut. The support block was moved into position to align the shaft. I mixed epoxy and put it into syringes to inject the voids around the tube.

After the epoxy had hardened, I removed the shaft and cut the tube flush with the hull bottom. The new liner would later be used in conjunction with the brass stuffing box screwed to the interi-

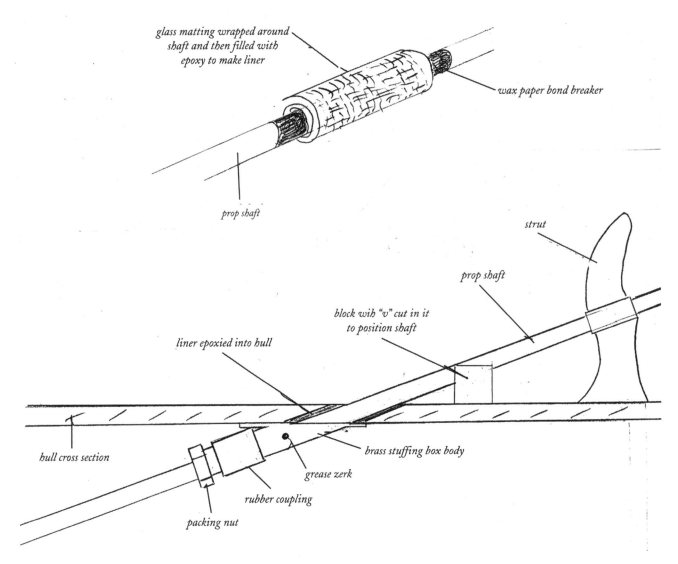

glass matting wrapped around
shaft and then filled with
epoxy to make liner

wax paper bond breaker

prop shaft

strut

prop shaft

block wih "v" cut in it
to position shaft

liner epoxied into hull

hull cross section

brass stuffing box body

grease zerk

rubber coupling

packing nut

A fiberglass tube was created that, when filled with grease, would help seal the prop shaft against water intrusion into the hull. It was installed in a carefully aligned hole and secured in place with epoxy.

or of the hull. A hole would be drilled and tapped in the brass body of the stuffing box and a grease zerk fitting would be threaded in. This permitted me to pump silicone grease into the stuffing box and liner to keep out water. It also lubricated the shaft. After sanding the new epoxy and glass bottom, several coats of copper bronze bottom paint were applied using rollers. At this point the hull was ready to be rolled upright.

A potential drawback to fiberglassing the boat's bottom was the fact that the bottom planks' interior surfaces were coated only by paint. In theory, there's still the chance for water to saturate the wood, which could allow the wood to swell and produce stress on the planking, frames, and epoxy bottom finish. A better solution would have been to totally remove the bottom planking and coat each plank and frame with epoxy on both sides. This would leave the water no path into the wood. That said, I've experienced no problems at all with the hull's bottom. In the years since relaunching, the only water I've had in the hull was due to a head gasket leak that left about a cup of water in the bilge. A box fan placed

The block beneath the prop shaft had a shallow groove cut into it and was used to help align the shaft.

in front of the open engine cover dries up any moisture.

Topsides and Staining

In January of 1995, over three years after I acquired the Chris-Craft, it was finally time to turn the boat back upright. The same method was once again employed to roll the hull. The 4 x 4s were once again strapped to the hull and the come-alongs were used to lift and lower. With the hull upright and pulled back on the trailer, I began replacing the gunwales using the re-sawn planks and router.

Once the gunwales were complete, I turned my attention to the front deck where all the bungs had been removed due to discoloration and poor condition. It was time to remove the old caulk from between the planks. I used the existing deck

plank screw locations to attach a board that acted as a guide for my circular saw. I attached the board so that the saw blade ran right down the center of a caulk line. I then moved the board over so that the blade ran down the center of the next, and so on, until all the caulk that could be removed was. Where space prevented using the saw, I used a razor knife. With the seams routed, new bungs were installed in the decks and gunwales, and a final sanding was given to the topsides.

It was now time to paint the bilge. I taped over anything that wasn't to have bilge paint on it and thoroughly cleaned the inside of the hull. Cleaning was accomplished by using a stiff brush, air compressor, and a vacuum with a soft brush attachment to clean up debris. I then applied two heavy coats of Chris-Craft burgundy bilge paint using an

The author removed his Chris-Craft's engine for rebuilding by a local shop. All hardware removed was placed in plastic bags and carefully labeled. The engine's absence made stripping, cleaning, and refinishing the boat's interior much easier.

airless sprayer purchased for a home improvement project. I used the airless sprayer because it lets less material permeate the air than a compressor and sprayer. This was important because of the confined space and limited ventilation.

Once the interior was painted, I thoroughly cleaned the hull and garage to eliminate dust. I prepared the garage using 10' x 30', 4-mil rolls of plastic. One side was stapled to 1" x 2" boards that were then screwed to the ceiling. I stapled the bottom edge along the floor to 2" x 4" boards that acted as weight to hold the plastic in place. This created walls on both sides of the hull to further control dust during staining and varnishing. I taped off the new bottom for protection.

Staining

I decided to divide the hull refinishing into two steps. Step one would be the hull sides including the transom. Step two would be the topsides. To separate the two areas, I ran KleenEdge easy release painter's tape, by Loparex, along the top edge of the rear deck and down the center of the stainless rub rails on the sides. When I purchased the mahogany planks from the restoration shop, the owner asked me if I'd decided on a stain color. I hadn't given thought to stain at the time. He had a half-dozen boats in the shop and suggested I take a look to see if any of the colors were to my liking. The color I chose turned out to be a 50/50 mixture of Pettit 7665 Dark Mahogany and 7666 Red Mahogany filler stains. Following staining directions from a July/August 1993 *Classic Boating* magazine article entitled "Color Me Brown" by Philip Ballantyne, I began.

Before each step — whether staining or applying varnish — I used a tack cloth to wipe down the surface. This is a cheap, quick, and easy step to aid in achieving a beautiful finish. I worked from the bow down the side, around the transom and back up the other side, using squares of burlap folded into pads to apply stain. I applied stain, which required constant stirring to keep the solids suspended, by rubbing in a circular motion, keeping a wet edge as I moved along. My dad followed behind, removing excess stain and polishing the surface by wiping in the direction of the grain with soft rags. When the sides of the hull had been stained, we protected them with masking tape and plastic so that the decks and gunwales could be stained in the same manner. The interior side planking, seat frames, and seat backs were stained in the shop on the bench. With staining complete, the next step was varnishing.

Varnishing

After reading many articles detailing techniques for brushing, roll and tipping, and spraying varnish, I went with the basic brush application. Later, after the boat's first season, I did try the roll and tip method to touch up the transom. Both methods worked; each has advantages and disadvantages. As when staining, I separated the hull into two pieces, doing sides first followed by the topsides. Preparation for each coat included cleaning the hull and wet mopping the floor. We wore hats, one-piece disposable painter suits, and respirators. Anything you can do to keep contaminates out of the air and off the work surface will pay dividends later.

The first several coats of varnish were brushed on, allowed to dry for 24 hours, and then lightly sanded using steel wool. We used a vacuum with a soft brush attachment and tack cloths to clean the surface between each coat. When I was confident the wood was sealed, I switched to 300-grit wet sandpaper between coats. This reduced dust, making cleanups easier, plus water helps prevent the sandpaper from clogging. Halogen spotlights (250-watt) on floor stands supplied lighting during the staining and varnishing phases. When positioned correctly, the lights shone on the surface wet from sanding and all surface defects were easy to see.

Eventually we applied 10 coats of Pettit 2015 Z Spar, Flagship Premium Exterior Marine Varnish. Historically, I've had difficulty getting good varnish results when working a flat surface, let alone the sides of a boat. The one thing in my favor was the time of year — winter. In the winter the air is naturally drier. Additionally, I heated my shop with wood, which helped dry the air. This shortened the varnish drying time. The topsides, interior planks, and seat components were done in the same manner. As these were all flat pieces, they were comparatively easy to varnish.

When it came to caulk the front and rear decks, I waited until I had applied half the varnish coats. I used a latex caulk — manufactured and recommended for this purpose — to fill the joints between the planks, followed by a wet finger to smooth it. A damp sponge cleaned off the excess. The remaining coats of varnish were then applied. The varnish tended to yellow the caulk so I taped around the caulk joints and used the water line paint to return them to a brilliant white. In hindsight, it might have been easier to apply the caulk after the final coat of varnish, saving the need for taping and painting. There have been no signs of adhesion problems.

Reassembly

With varnishing complete, the task of reassembling the boat finally began. Normally this would be an easy task, but since I'd purchased what was basically a bare hull with boxes of parts, I hadn't seen many of them in place. A trip to an antique boat show some years earlier had gotten me several rolls of pictures of a 1951 18-foot Chris-Craft Sportsman equipped with a K motor, one year older than mine but nearly identical. With these in hand, I was able to verify hardware positioning, the style of missing hardware, and even the shape of the windshield, missing when purchased.

Over the years I'd cleaned and polished the

Here is the boat's 95 hp Chris-Craft K engine, based on a Hercules block, before restoration.

various pieces of brass (which I then sprayed with lacquer), chrome-plated brass, and stainless for the day they'd be remounted. I had purchased boxes of new chrome-plated or stainless mounting screws. Interior planks and seat frames were the first to go in. The steering wheel/gearbox assembly, dash instruments, and switches followed, along with new wiring including a new fuse block located behind the dash.

The pieces I'd removed were reinstalled using drawings located in their storage bags or from notes. I made a windshield template out of masonite and took it to a glass shop where the new windshield was made from safety glass. When it came time to rebuild the engine, a neighbor told me of a mechanic just down the road that worked on everything from diesel semis to old

tractors. I arranged a meeting and was pleased to find he was familiar with the Hercules block on which the 95-hp Chris-Craft K was based. He had experience on this vintage of block but from tractors, not boats. He took a look at it and said it wouldn't be a problem but I'd be responsible for the hard-to-find parts.

I shopped for missing hardware, engine parts, and anything needing replacement on eBay, at antique shops, or from parts dealers. The two most expensive components — found on eBay, for a grand total of $400 — were the oil pressure/amp meter gauge and the tachometer. Both had been professionally restored with rebuilt movements, repainted faces, and re-chromed bezels. A surprising find at an antique store was the rear mast fitting, including an original lens plus a spare 12" x 13" bronze prop.

I found eBay to be an excellent source of information as well as parts. I purchased a CD containing all specifications for the boat and motor, parts lists, operation manuals, maintenance manuals, service bulletins, and a manual entitled *Specifications and Adjustment Tolerances for Chris-Craft In-Line 4 & 6 Cylinder Marine Engines*, which was of particular interest to the mechanic.

About halfway through the boat's reassembly, the engine was completed. The eventual work list for the rebuild read as follows:

"Completely disassembled engine and pressure cleaned block and all parts, crank ground to .020, new set of main bearings and rod bearings, cylinders bored to .030, #2 cylinder sleeved and bored to .030, connecting rods reconditioned, new pistons and rings, installed new hardened

valve seats and all new exhaust valves, new freeze plugs, complete gasket set, new front engine seal, plugs, wires, coil, points, condenser, distributor cap and coil."

I took the starter, generator, carburetor, and fuel pump to local shops to be rebuilt. The oil pump, water pump, distributor and transmission were in good condition and required cleaning only. The various parts and the final assembly were then painted Ford Blue. The engine was successfully test run prior to reinstallation while hanging from a chain hoist in the mechanic's shop. Because the engine shop had a large A-frame, I towed the boat there to reinstall the engine. This was quickly done and the engine bolted back into position. With engine in place, and some $3,500 spent, we could install the stuffing box, drive shaft, and strut. The fuel line, with a new inline filter, throttle, choke, oil pressure

A restored vintage engine is a showpiece in its own right. The Chris-Craft Model K, finished in blue enamel, runs smoothly.

The 1952 Chris-Craft Sportsman didn't originally have such luxurious upholstery, however, the author opted to replace the factory-correct, thinly padded blue seats with thicker foam versions covered in the pleated, burgundy material seen here.

gauge tube, and wiring were put in place and connected. We installed a new six-volt battery and tested the lights.

In the beginning of the project, I decided to upgrade the upholstery and flooring. The original, thinly-padded, blue seat-back covers and loose base pads were replaced with thicker foam padding of a different color and pattern. After looking through boating magazines and books, I decided on a pleated pattern and burgundy color. I took the pictures to a local upholstery shop, picked a color from samples, and delivered the boat for installation. Upholstery came to a grand total of $1,800.

Upholstery now complete, I ordered and installed a matching burgundy marine carpet. The carpet came in a roll that I laid out on the shop floor upside down. I transferred measurements from the floor of the boat to the carpet, with a little extra on the sides to be trimmed to fit once it was lying in the boat. I then stapled it in place with stainless staples and trimmed the excess. A trim strip of mahogany, screwed into place down the sides, provided a nice finished look.

With the boat basically complete, I added fuel to the tank, and attempted to start the engine using a garden hose connected to the water pump. Since the engine had been rebuilt, the six-volt battery wouldn't turn the starter fast enough. I called the mechanic who'd performed the overhaul. He came, checked connections and the ignition system, and found no problems. He recommended upgrading to a 12-volt battery for the starting solenoid. With the higher voltage battery it didn't take much coaxing to bring the K to life. The mechanic made carburetor and timing adjustments and we left the motor running for a couple hours of break-in time. We also fixed several cooling system leaks, one from what appeared to be an additional mounting hole, but turned out to be a drain plug for the block. The threads were in poor condition but I was able to run a 1/4" x 20 tap into it and then installed a brass plug purchased at a local hardware store.

RELAUNCH

When the great day finally arrived to refloat the *Vintage Vixen*, there wasn't a lot left to chance. For the initial launch, the engine cover was left in the garage and several floorboards were either removed or put down loosely so that I could easily check for leaks. The pre-launch checks were performed, a half-dozen pumps of grease added to the stuffing box, the trailer backed into the water, and the boat was floated off. I performed a quick check for leaks and found a wet spot under the fuel tank. (Due to the steepness of the ramp, a cup of water was pushed back through the auto-bailer. When I mentioned this to other classic boat owners at a boat show, I was advised to take the bailer out or plug it, as it's responsible for sinking many a boat. Since my boat lacks an automatic bilge pump, it could sink if the water level in the hull exceeded the top of the bailer. I plugged the bailer.)

I started the engine. I located the neutral position of the gearbox and verified that cooling water exited from the exhaust pipe. After several short test runs, checking for leaks and engine operation, we installed the engine cover and floorboards. The fun began in earnest.

IN RETROSPECT

When I initially purchased the boat, I knew this would be a multi-year project. However, I didn't think it would take 11 years! Having a family, job, and home didn't leave a lot of time or money for the restoration. But things usually slowed down in the winter months, allowing for a little more progress each year. Researching techniques, materials, and finding imaginative ways of getting tasks done with limited equipment was as much fun as doing the work. I tried many new techniques — rolling over a hull, glass and epoxy coating, reproducing hull pieces using worn or broken originals as templates, deck caulk removal, and caulk installation. None were extremely difficult but all required some study and planning.

There were many high points during the restoration, such as plank replacement, staining, and varnishing. A low point was when the hull wasn't touched for 18 months and I wondered if I should have ever started. Do I regret the experience? Not at all. Would I ever tackle another restoration project again? Only if it was something extremely unique or interesting — something to push my skills and create a conversation piece.

When budgeting for the project, I estimated that the cost of the materials would be under $10,000. Since this was a hobby we enjoyed working on, I decided not to track expenses. I couldn't even begin to guess at the number of man-hours invested. Once again, it really didn't matter since my dad and I enjoyed working on it together, usually on Wednesday nights. As in any undertaking of this nature, a patient, understanding partner is a must. My wife Terri was there for the highs and lows. She ultimately convinced me that contributing to this book would be a fitting testimonial to the project.

THE BOAT TODAY

The original intent of the restoration was to have a boat to use on sunny summer days for a slow cruise on the river. I didn't intend to take it to shows. However, in July of 2004 we took the *Vintage Vixen* to the 13th Annual Minocqua Antique & Classic Boat Show in Minocqua, Wisconsin. This was the first time since the boat was finished that I'd been to a show. It was the perfect time to see how our work stacked up to

Who can resist the iconic look of a beautifully varnished Chris-Craft? Perseverance and attention to detail resulted in a show-piece that rewarded the author for his patience.

others. We were quite happy to find the boat was comparable to many there, several of which had been restored or maintained by shops. Meeting and talking to other boat owners was great.

As for its performance, with two or three people onboard the boat planes easily and handles well. If four people and gear are on board, getting on plane is more difficult. This summer I will experiment with different props in order to overcome this problem. Re-chroming the hardware is also on a future to-do list, along with an additional coat of varnish over the newly painted name and registration numbers. I hope to be able to remove the 12-volt battery after the engine gets a few more hours on it and loosens up. In the summer of 2005 the boat took the place of honor in our boathouse, replacing my 18-foot Baja. From this vantage point, she can more easily gain

access to the water for an early evening cruise. After all the years of work we're looking forward to enjoying the finished product.

BOAT SPECS

Brand	Chris-Craft
Model	Sportsman
Year Built	1952
Length x Beam x Draft	18′5″ x 6′4″ x 1′6″
Weight	2,100 lbs.
Engine	95-hp Chris-Craft K
Advertised Speed	32 mph
Prop	12 x 13 Michigan
Original list price	$3,047
Purchase price 1992	$2,500

PRODUCTS AND SUPPLIERS

Following is a list of materials and suppliers used during the restoration:

Gougeon Brothers:
- "Basic Application Techniques" video tape
- West System 105 Epoxy Resin and 205 Hardener
- West System 403 microfibers
- 60-Inch glass fabric
- Miscellaneous foam rollers, mixing pots, syringes, plastic squeegees

Chesapeake Marine Fasteners:
- Brass screws as needed
- 3/8-inch plug cutter
- #5, #7 and #8 drill, countersink, stop, assemblies

Wooden Boat Shop:
- Pettit Paste Wood Filler — 7665 Dark Mahogany and 7666 Red Mahogany
- Pettit 2015 Z Spar Flagship Premium Exterior Marine Varnish
- Interlux 310 White (boot top)
- Chris-Craft burgundy bilge paint
- Copper bronze bottom paint

SUMMARY TOOL LIST
- 10" Craftsman Contractor table saw
- 12" Delta planner
- 12" Dewalt compound miter saw
- Jigsaw
- Ryobi detail sander
- Floor standing drill press
- 1 1/4-hp router and router table with a variety of bits
- Wagner airless sprayer
- 5-hp air compressor
- Grizzly Dust collection system
- Cordless and corded drills
- 1/4-sheet electric sander
- Belt sander
- Tabletop disk/belt sander
- ShopVac
- Come-alongs
- Laser and tripod
- Various hand tools

About the Author: Born in 1956 in Milwaukee, Wisconsin, Russ Ballenger attended public schools, including Boy's Technical High School, before graduating from the Milwaukee School of Engineering with Associate degrees in Computer Engineering and Electronic Communications. In 1981, while a Field Engineer for a computer equipment manufacturer, he moved to Stevens Point in central Wisconsin where he purchased a home on an 11-mile stretch of water above the Biron dam. Russ says his shop skills came from being brought up in a home with a basement workshop and a dad in building maintenance. During the restoration project, Russ's dad Jim assisted with a second set of hands, eyes and ideas. Russ and his wife Terri have three children.

3

A Classic Daysailer

BY TIM HEALEY

Mention the name John Alden and most folks think of Malabar schooners and a long succession of cruising yachts and ocean racers. That said, Alden's staff of immensely talented designers also produced an impressive group of one-design racers and daysailers. The charming little boat that is the subject of this chapter was created by the Boston design office of John Alden in July 1931. Design 346-B was officially referred to as a centerboard sailing dinghy and was distinct from the earlier, larger, and better-known O Boat. The fun potential of a boat like this far outstrips its diminutive size. For a devoted skipper, the trailerable Design 346-B offers the potential for a lifetime of little adventures. It is believed that five boats were built to this design, every one of them named for Gilbert & Sullivan operettas popular during the early '30s. The author of this chapter was fortunate enough to learn his boat's original name, a bonus that, as the following makes clear, was entirely unexpected. Note that plans for this boat, and other classic Alden designs, remain available. They may be ordered from: John G. Alden, 89 Commercial Wharf, Boston, MA 02110. (www.aldendesigns.com)

My old wooden sailboat, *Ruddigore*, came to me by way of my father. I bought the boat from him for two dollars in June of 2000. That summer I was suffering from "deep-draft-itis". My 25-foot, steel-hull, full-keel sailboat, designed by Peterson Shipbuilding in Sturgeon Bay, Wisconsin, was sitting in its cradle under cover because the water level in Lake Michigan had dropped to the point where I could not navigate my way in or out of my sailing club's channel. This was the second year during which we'd experienced sporadic low water levels and, in the back of my mind, I found myself wishing for a centerboard boat with the flexibility to handle the crazy Lake Michigan water level fluctuations. I had spent some time crewing on a Lightning during the previous summer and the experience made a strong impression on me. It was fun to be down, close to the water again, versus seated in the safe, stable cockpit of my heavy cruiser. In fact, the Lightning reminded me of my boyhood days learning to sail on *Ruddigore*. Heeling over, instant tiller feedback, wind puff acceleration, and light air performance — those were things my cruiser didn't do well.

My Dad, Tim Sr., originally bought *Ruddigore* from his dentist for one dollar back in the mid-'70s. Dad rescued the boat from an old boathouse on Lake Michigamme in the central part of Michigan's Upper Peninsula. The lake is essentially a duplicate to the lake setting for the movie On Golden Pond. As for the boat, "rescued" was an apt term — it was in pretty bad shape. There were holes in the hull and the mast was bent like a noodle. What's more, the boat was covered by about 30 coats of paint on everything — hull, seats, fittings, deck, even the spars. I was just 10 years old when the boat entered our family, but I always remembered the remark made by Harry Gall, a friend of my dad's who helped us haul the boat out of the boathouse. After helping winch the boat up a steep hill and load it onto a utility trailer, Harry said, "The owner of the boat should be paying us to take it off his hands."

Little did my dad know he was buying a boat created by the famed design office of John Alden. Dad simply wanted a daysailer he could use on our local Teal Lake in Negaunee, Michigan. It was not until several years later that we learned about *Ruddigore*'s pedigree. My dad fixed up the boat with some help from me. I can still remember scraping gooey coats of zip-stripped paint off the hull. I also remember the stuff really burns the skin. My mother Carol also assisted with the restoration by helping to lay fiberglass over the outside of the hull. Dad taught me how to sail on the boat and we used it for four or five summers. Eventually the effort required to row out to the boat and bail out the rainwater and leaking centerboard became too much.

By 1984 I had become interested in old cars, girls, and then college, while dad spent his time on the water fishing rather than sailing. *Ruddigore* spent the next 15 years under a tarp, parked in the woods, providing a great nesting place for various squirrels and mice. When I expressed some interest in the old boat during the summer of 2000, Tim Sr. was pretty happy to see it out of his yard, and

at the same time happy to see it stay in the family. He jokes to this day that he doubled his money on the boat when he sold it to me for two bucks.

After I decided that I was ready to take on the project, my dad helped me make some quick roller and bunk adjustments to an old 14-foot fishing boat trailer so I could transport *Ruddigore*. I towed the old boat to my house in Green Bay, Wisconsin, where it would end up occupying the west stall of my two-car garage for the next three years. After owning and working on several boats ranging from catamarans to my 25-footer (which I sold due to its too-deep draft), I knew that having this project 20 feet away from my family room, and under a roof, would give me the best chance for success. I had learned the hard way that working on a boat at a marina, or even worse on a mooring, really cuts into the actual work time. Too much time is wasted traveling and lining up materials and tools — and then there are weather issues!

What's more, with two young daughters I knew that being able to supervise play in the driveway while still getting something done in the garage would promote the good graces of my better half, Amy. My truck, however, was banished from the garage. It would be buried under snow in the winter and liberally spotted with tree sap in the summer. Dad reminded me that when he did his repair work in the '70s, he did it in a one-stall garage which meant our family station wagon sat outside all winter. Considering that Negaunee regularly receives over 200 inches of snow, that was quite a sacrifice.

When I got the boat home, I knew that I really needed to look it over and formulate a game plan. Since I couldn't sail my cruising boat, I hoped to get *Ruddigore* in the water quickly. My first thought was to remove the centerboard trunk, rebuild it, and then do additional restoration work while using the boat. I remembered that the last time the boat was in the water the joint between the centerboard trunk bedlogs and the

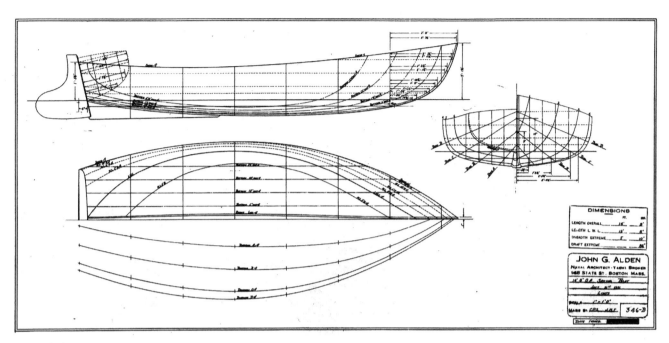

The lines of author Healey's classic daysailer were created by the John Alden office in the 1930s. The boat's modest deadrise (relatively flat bottom) and a hull that is basically double-ended below the waterline suggest a stable little craft that will slip easily through the water.

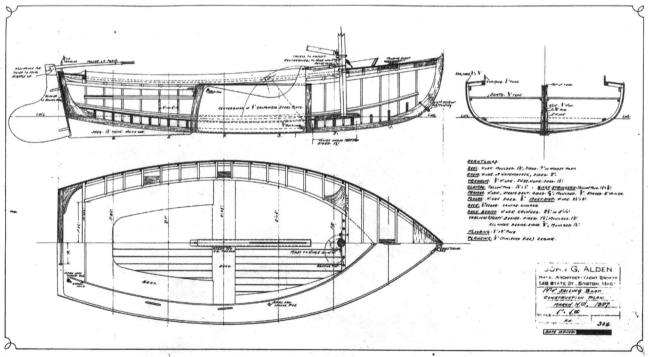

The construction drawings for Alden design 346-B are still available and were of much use to the author during his restoration project. The ready availability of such plans makes practical new construction of this and other Alden classics.

keel leaked like a sieve. I recall my Dad saying that it required both of us to take out *Ruddigore* — "one to sail and one to bail." After a little poking, I found the trunk logs were punky. There was no need to use the old ice pick method here: I could dent the white oak with my bare fingernails!

Before I got started with the centerboard trunk replacement, I wanted to know how that part of the boat had been assembled. It was difficult to really tell how the various components that made up the bottom of the boat fit together because our fiberglass job covered the areas adjacent to the slot. At that point, I contacted the Alden office in Boston and was delighted to learn that they could supply me with a full set of the original plans done back in the '30s. The Alden office also had a sail plan and list of specifications for all the materials that made up the boat. I was thrilled with all the data available on my 69-year-old boat and they were thrilled to hear that I had one of their vintage boats and was planning to restore it.

I began the centerboard trunk replacement phase by gathering up some neighbors to flip the hull. Six of us were able to manage without doing any damage or straining any backs. My neighbors had a myriad of questions about the project. They are normally amused with the do-it-yourself projects I work on around the house, but this one was obviously different.

After the hull was turned over and exposed, I could see a few "zipper" cracks in the fiberglass around the centerboard slot. I decided to use a Dremel tool to cut a rectangular-shaped hole through the glass about two inches wider than the centerboard slot. I was a bit surprised at how easily the glass pealed off the keel; the wood was spongy enough that the glass came off with some wood fiber attached to it. With the glass off, I could see the wood plugs covering the screw heads that held the trunk in place. Everything appeared to match up with the drawing details.

Trying to remove the first of the 22 bronze

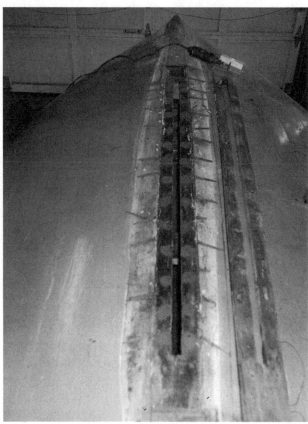

The centerboard slot would prove to be one of the more complex aspects of the Alden daysailer's restoration. Here is the slot after the boat's rebuilding. The plank keel, cut out to permit movement of the board itself, is ready for installation.

screws holding the trunk in place did not go well. First, I stripped the slot out and then broke the head off. The next two screws suffered the same result. Getting desperate, I then used a 3/4-inch hole saw to drill through the keel and around each of the 22 screws that held the trunk in place. This meant that I could actually separate the mechanical connection between the keel and bedlogs. After all the keel screws were out, I needed to go under the hull and remove the angled screws that connected the oak floors to the side of the trunk. With a little wiggling and some light prying, the trunk was loose — a momentous occasion at the time.

With winter setting in, I moved the centerboard trunk rebuild phase down to my basement. Taking the case apart was not difficult. I was care-

The original cedar centerboard trunk was in fine shape. When the author counted the rings in the 16-inch wide boards, he learned they had come from a tree that was 300 years old.

ful to keep as much of the original wood intact as possible because I was going to be making patterns for the replacement pieces. With the trunk removed, I found the bedlogs were in worse shape than I had been able to tell from the outside. The inside surface of the white oak was either missing or simply a honeycomb of wood. This rot was not present at all in the cedar trunk sides; in fact the cedar was in great shape. As I looked over the inside face of the cedar, I was impressed by the size of the tree that these 16-inch wide boards must have come from. I then looked over the end grain and I was amazed to count 300 growth rings. These two cedar boards had been cut from a tree that had been around since the 1600s!

The excellent condition of the cedar components gave me hope. The oak deterioration had caused me to question the integrity of all the wood in the boat. The major concern I had was the hull planking itself. I kept my fingers crossed that the cedar planking beneath the fiberglass would be in as good condition as the trunk sides. I consulted the WoodenBoat website, which has a great forum for building and repair questions. By doing some keyword searches, I found a few stories of success from those who had glassed over wooden carvel-built hulls; most were stories of failure. After sharing the fact that the increasingly leaky boat had spent many summers moored on a local lake filling with rainwater, I found myself trading messages with folks who couldn't believe the hull wasn't "mush". Most of those I heard from suggested that a hull, fiberglassed on the outside, had no right to be anything other than rotten. A few "experts" told me that my boat was "wrecked" and would make a good flower pot or play set for my kids. My reaction to this feedback was discouragement mixed with a little insult. That said, I did have to admit that my initial plan — to get sailing soon — was clearly unrealistic. The little Alden was going to be a bigger project than I'd imagined.

As I worked on rebuilding the centerboard trunk that first winter, I started to ask myself if I really wanted to do a simple repair job to the fiberglass around the centerboard slot or restore the *Ruddigore* back to her original status as a "wooden" boat. I now grew to believe that I would be doing the boat a favor by adhering the boat to its original construction as closely as possible. Then I could officially join the unofficial club of wooden boat owners! A *Ruddigore* with a fiberglassed bottom would never be quite the same thing. Once again, I consulted the WoodenBoat forum to seek some input on stripping fiberglass off a cedar hull. I received mixed opinions. Ultimately I decided to go for it, based on how easily the glass had peeled off the keel area and on the comments of one forum writer who said that fiberglass resin used in the mid- '70s wasn't nearly as tenacious at bonding to wood as modern epoxy. Returning to the garage, I started to cut a little more fiberglass off around the keel and found that it did literally pull off in small sheets. Eventually I got into a rhythm by cutting and pulling at certain angles. It reminded me of peeling an orange. Very little cedar fiber was coming off with the glass. That was a big plus for I worried about ruining the boat for good if chunks of the cedar planking started coming off.

I spent a few days carefully peeling my boat. Fortunately it was cold outside so an old sweatshirt, leather gloves, and safety glasses weren't too uncomfortable. After I got all the glass off, I threw all the clothes I'd worn during the process away as my wife didn't want shards of fiberglass rolling around in the washer for an eternity. I also did a thorough job of vacuuming my garage.

Peeling off the fiberglass on the boat's bottom revealed cedar planks that were still in excellent condition, but some 80 hours was spent removing glass residue and returning the cedar to its natural state.

Fiberglass strands are extremely itchy when they contact the skin. Worse, they seemed to drift everywhere, including all over our yellow lab who then required many baths. To this day I occasionally find a little blue splinter of the fiberglass in my driveway and I can't count how many times I've cleaned it with a broom and leaf blower.

Now that the glass was off, I turned to sanding off the resin that had soaked through the glass and still adhered to the cedar planking. The hard resin came off fairly easily, but I soon learned that the cedar planking was extremely soft in comparison. It was very easy to get carried away trying to sand all the blue resin off while lots of cedar sawdust was flying as well. I caught myself many times chasing resin with my sander at the cost of cedar, so I started using a house siding scraper instead. This worked very well. When used carefully, the scraper collided with the resin, sending it flying while removing little or no wood.

After 80 hours of scraping, I had a cedar-planked wooden boat in the garage. This was great progress for it meant that I had returned the hull to its natural state. My plan was to dry-sail the boat — keeping it on a trailer when not in use — rather than leaving it on a mooring or at a dock for the summer. This meant that I now faced a decision about how to deal with the seams in the bottom planking. If I kept the traditional cotton seams, I would have no choice but to suffer from the required swell cycle each time I launched the boat. This would regularly stress the hull. At the same time, I knew of a few other carvel-type hulls that were being successfully dry-sailed with epoxy seams. A few people on the WoodenBoat forum said that this was not a good idea for a traditional carvel hull. But I heard from others that the technique would work fine on a well-built smaller boat if done properly. Properly was the key word. To be successful, there could be no shortcuts in preparation.

I now set about the tedious task of cleaning out all the seams. I used a utility knife with regular blades and carpet cutter blades. The carpet blades have a hook on the end, which helps grab hold of the cotton deep in the seam. My miniature version of an old-fashioned schooner reefing hook worked very well. I occasionally needed to use a Dremel tool to grind out resin that had soaked into the cotton filler more than 20 years ago, but this was not needed often. I now found that one of my most useful tools was also one of the cheapest: a bent tang file. I got the idea from a *WoodenBoat* article. I heated the tang (handle) of an ordinary metal file with a torch and then used vise grips and a 1/2-inch pipe to put a 90-degree hook in the end. This tool also came in handy for picking out small chunks of old fiberglass resin and the dried Gluvit that had been put in the trunk area over the years to stop leaks.

The file was the perfect width and, with the end ground to a point, it also allowed me to get all the old materials out of the seam while not pushing through. The technique was to clean the sides of the seam to their full depth but not create a gap that the epoxy would run through. The bent tang file and I became very good friends over the

After hours of work with a utility knife with a carpet cutter blade and a Dremel tool, the boat's seams were clean and ready for treatment with an epoxy sealer followed by caulking with thickened epoxy.

course of many weeknights. We listened to every Gordon Lightfoot CD I owned, which is every one he's ever released. This whole exercise was repetitive and a little mind-numbing, but attention to the details at this stage was critical to the outcome of the project. The last thing I wanted was to go through all this work and have a seam or two give me problems because the epoxy adhered to some leftover paint or caulk. Progress seemed slow to my family and friends who didn't see much change through this stage. It seemed that only I had an appreciation for this drab but very necessary task. I completed the seam cleaning by rubbing folded sandpaper through every inch of every seam and then sucking out the debris with a shop vac. By the time the seams were clean, I had spent about 100 hours on them.

Once I was satisfied that the seams were perfectly cleaned out, I did a quick gut check by setting up a halogen light under the boat one night and then turning out the overhead lights in my garage. Little slivers of light lit up the ceiling like a disco. My little girls thought it looked cool but I was a little surprised at how much light was penetrating my old hull; in daylight it looked like I had preserved most of the wood-to-wood contact deep in the seams. If that much light was making its way through, I knew epoxy would run right through it. Taping the inside would be necessary as I didn't want to have epoxy running through the seams and getting on the inside surfaces of the boat and garage floor. I tipped the boat up on its side so I had access to the inside for taping.

This is the point where I bought some Smith's CPES (clear penetrating epoxy sealer). This product came highly recommended for prepping wood for epoxy work. I had spent a lot of time reading testimonials on the internet. Smith's CPES is a two-part formula of very watery epoxy. The product's thinness lets it penetrate the wood cells and preserves them while keeping the properties of the wood itself, i.e. no brittleness.

Smith's other claim for the product is its adhesion properties when varnish or epoxy is applied over it. This was especially important to me, seeing as I was essentially turning my carvel (basket-like) hull into more of a monocular (egg-like) hull. I coated the inside bevels of all the seams with the CPES using a regular bristle brush. As I did so, I told myself that *Ruddigore*'s seams had not seen the light of day since the 1930s and would probably never be exposed again. With the CPES applied, I next spent many hours applying 3M blue painters tape to the inside of all the seams. This taping had to be tight, without any gaps that epoxy could leak through. Working around the hull's oak frames with the tape was a little harder than I had anticipated.

Next, I ordered some empty caulking tubes from Jamestown Distributors. I planned to mix up batches of West System epoxy with 404 adhesive filler and then pour it into the caulking tubes for gunning into the seams. This technique worked

The hull was turned on its side so that the author could check to see that the planking seams were perfectly free of debris. Tape was then applied over the inside of the seams to prevent the epoxy sealer and caulking from running right through the seams and onto the interior of the planks.

well. Each tube held enough epoxy to do about two seams per mixed batch, the limiting factor being the epoxy working time. I let the seams sit 24 hours before moving on to the next set of two, cocking the boat so the seams pointed as straight up as possible for application. To support the hull during this process, I cut different lengths of 2 x 4s and used them to prop up the hull, working from port to starboard. The flared bow near the waterline was the most difficult area in which to keep the epoxy from running out and across the planks.

After I had filled all the seams and removed the tape, I turned my attention to fairing the hull. Doing a good job at this point was also vital. I planned to seal the entire hull with CPES followed by a coat of epoxy resin and, finally, a coat of epoxy mixed with 422 barrier coat additive. One of the few tools I had to purchase was a Porter Cable random orbital sander. This sander proved

invaluable for the hull fairing. I used it on just about everything that needed sanding. I would estimate I went through over 100 discs each of 60- and 80-grit sandpaper. I'm sure my neighbors must have gotten sick of listening to the hum of the sander night after night but I never heard any complaints. I used a 3M dust mask even though the sander had a collection canister. Despite the latter, my CD player ultimately burned out from all the dust in the garage. After the orbital sander, I used a two-foot long sanding board with 80-grit sheets to assure fair lines. During the sanding, I used ear protection on and off. I needed to take breaks due to my hand getting tingly after long sanding sessions.

With sanding complete, I coated the whole hull with CPES. Then I applied West System epoxy over the hull with a tight-nap foam roller. I remember that during the epoxy coating process a few onlookers commented that they couldn't

With the hull seams sealed and the bottom ready for painting, holes were bored that would later accept the fasteners used to attach the keel plank.

believe I was going to paint the boat. Granted, the cedar hull did look stunning, all shiny and bright through the epoxy, but this was no strip-built canoe. I knew that a proper paint scheme would be icing on the cake. After sorting through just about every traditional boat magazine, article, and website I could find, I decided on off-white and green, with a sand accent color for the deck and floorboards.

I covered the whole hull with a coat of two-part primer and then wet- sanded with 200-grit sandpaper. I repeated this two-step process. I then measured off the waterline according to the original Alden drawings, using a combination of a nylon string loop and a series of pencil marks. I painted the bottom with Interlux Brightside Sea Green #4247, with a hefty dose of flattener mixed in. I didn't want my old wooden boat looking like a glossy fiberglass production hull. I was really happy with the way the Brightside smoothed out as it cured. It made my pretty novice paint brush job look almost sprayed on.

From the waterline up, I painted with Brightside Hatteras White #4218, again with flattener mixed in. I knew the white would keep the hull cooler, not that I was that concerned about hull temperatures living in Wisconsin, but I had read that dark colors can really make planking

The mahogany transom was carefully masked off during the painting of the hull and a small score was made to yield a crisp line between the varnished transom and the painted ends of the hull planks.

heat up and potentially stress the epoxy joints. I wanted the white to be just different enough so it didn't look too white. In other words, I didn't want a 1930s vintage boat with an icy cool, brilliant or fluorescent white hull. Instead, I wanted it to look a little bit antique. I was careful to keep the mahogany transom masked off during the entire painting process. Using a Dremel tool, I made a small score in the mahogany transom planking about 3/4 inches inside the wineglass shape. That line is where the paint would transition to varnish.

I could see real progress now — a complete solid hull, painted, and looking sharp. At this point I needed to spruce up my old fishing boat trailer so I could flip the boat over and get on with the rest of the project. This was the best time to get the trailer redone because I had unencumbered access. I didn't feel the need to do anything fancy, but I wanted the bunks to fit nice and tight, giving my hull proper support during the extended periods it would spend atop them. I moved the trailer into the second stall of the garage where I did the wire brushing, priming, painting, and bunk shaping. I used Rustoleum for the trailer frame, fenders, and wheels and found that the colors were an almost perfect match for the Interlux colors I'd used on the boat.

I didn't lollygag with this part of the project as my wife's van was now parked out in the driveway. My entire garage was a boat shop. Although I might think that this was the way it ought to be, my normally understanding spouse had her own ideas. Still, she was such a good sport that she lent some of her artistic talent to paint my last name on the trailer tongue in fancy letters, per my sailing club's rules.

By now, it had been two years since my neighbors had helped me turn the boat over and, at last, I needed them to return to set the completed hull on the refurbished trailer. Of course, I was a little more nervous this time and was anxious to avoid any missteps, scratches, or bumps. Not wanting to take any chances, I recruited a few extra hands, including neighbor Bill Burnham who brought a calming influence to the effort. Everything went smoothly and we shared a few beers afterwards. I was excited to have the boat sitting upright on the trailer and happy that it fit the bunks very well. Now the deck and the inside really stuck out like a sore thumb in comparison to the finished hull.

The previous summer I had stripped the deck of its original canvas covering prior to turning the boat upside down. Now I had to remove the 300 staples and tacks that had secured the canvas. I used needle nose pliers and an old office staple puller. Given the apparent success of my method for restoring the hull, I decided not to recover the small foredeck and narrow side decks with canvas. Instead, I chose to redo the deck using the same basic method I'd used on the hull. I routed out the deck seams and then filled them with epoxy. Unlike the hull, however, I topped off the deck areas with an Interlux product called Interdeck. The cream-colored Interdeck paint came premixed with a sandlike texture built in. I tested it out on a small scrap of wood and liked the look and feel but not the color. The stock cream color was too yellow; I had more of a sand color in my mind.

I decided to go to my local Home Depot and look through their color chips. Eventually I selected a color called Sierra Vista by Berh. Who knew there were so many shades of beige? The paint mixer did a nice job estimating how much colorant to add to the cream Interdeck to match the stock Sierra Vista. He needed to be right because I planned to use Berh exterior porch paint in that exact color on the floor boards.

Next, I decided to finish up the interior plank scraping that I had started the summer before. There was very little room for a power sanding tool between the many frames and floors, so this

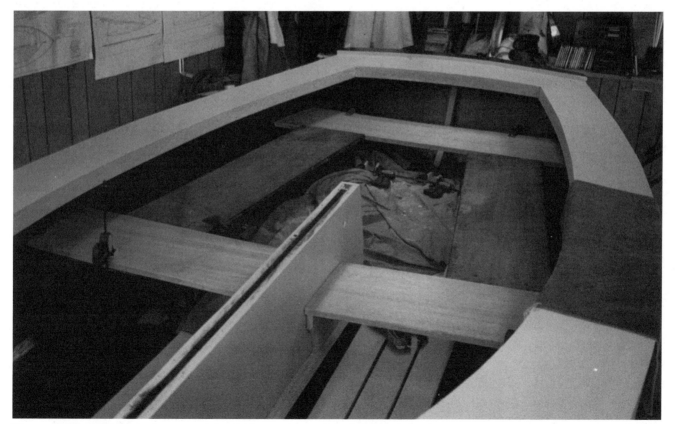

The canvas that had originally covered the decks was not replaced. Instead, the deck seams were routed and filled with epoxy. Then the deck was painted.

was a manual scrape and sand job. The only positive I could come up with for this arduous task was the fact that I could again listen to the stereo. Lightfoot was back on the speakers and, with a little additional help from Jimmy Buffet, I pressed on. I convinced myself that the inside needed to be really clean because I was going to coat it with CPES as well. It was while scraping the floorboards that I made a discovery of sorts. On the underside of two of the cedar slat floorboard assemblies, I found, written in pencil, the boat's name: *Ruddigore*. This had been written by the builder 70 years earlier.

When I eventually got to brushing on the penetrating epoxy, I was reminded of the fact that CPES was pretty potent stuff. One evening a few mosquitoes and flies literally dropped out of the air above me from the fumes, even though I had the garage doors open and a fan blowing. In hindsight, I should have used a better respirator myself.

Because the garage was not heated, when fall set in I moved my winter project activities back down to the basement. I worked on stripping and refinishing all the teak on the boat: the cleats, tiller, and coamings. I also stripped and refinished the fiberglass-covered oak rudder. I was able to sneak my 21-foot long mast and the 12-foot boom in through a basement window. Both spars, made of sitka spruce, were in good shape except for a small section at the base of the mast where, I suspect, standing water had led to rot. To repair them, I cut out the damaged center section and laminated some new spruce using six layers of 3/16-inch stock.

I also cleaned up the bronze hardware that winter. By April, 2003 I was at the point were I needed to make lists of items in order to bring the project to an early summer launch date. In doing so, I drastically underestimated the time and money required to get everything wrapped up. Fitting out was extensive and this was just a small daysailer. I can only imagine what would be required on a large cruiser. I placed many orders for various necessities including new stainless standing rigging, tarred marline, screws, bolts, blocks, etc. Jamestown Distributors was an excellent source for all of the fasteners on the project. In fitting out the boat with hardware, I now added a block to the centerboard pennant in order to give my girls a chance to handle the 70-pound, 1/4-inch steel plate. Even today I remember what it was like struggling to raise that board as a boy.

When it came time to rig the boat I had some good luck. By accident, while traveling on business in the Seattle area, I discovered traditional-looking line. The Wooden Boat Foundation, located in Port Townsend, sells a buff polyester rope by English Braids that looks and feels like old-fashioned, weathered, three-strand cotton line. It is beige in color, soft on the hands, and looks perfect on a vintage boat. I also sourced a lot of specialty bronze fittings from Bristol Bronze. I was

Cleats, traveler, and the boat's various hardware pieces represented a project within a project, but the end result contributed to the boat's good looks and function.

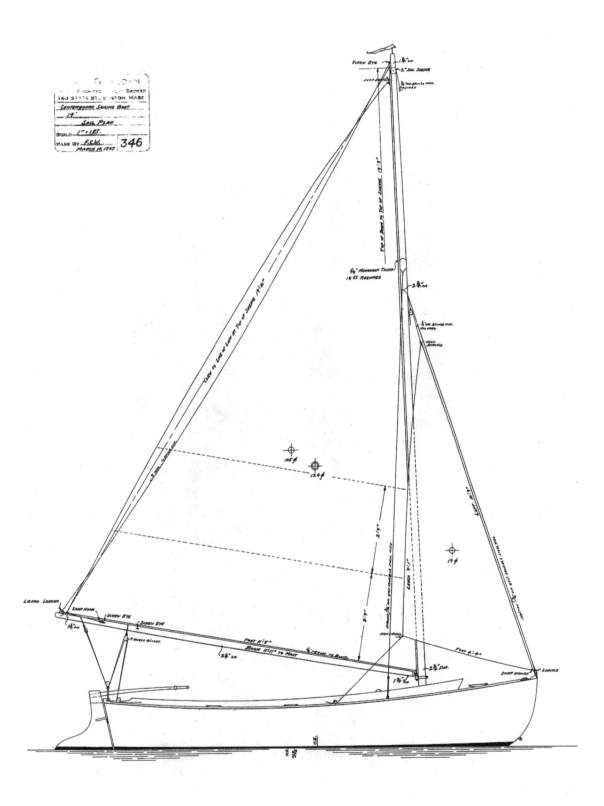

The boat's original spars and sail plan helped the sail maker produce sails that fit properly and contribute to outstanding performance.

able to substitute some of the missing bronze parts with those from a Herreshoff 12 1/2. Bristol sold me a new bow eye, stem strap, traveler rod, along with rudder pintles and gudgeons. Many of these parts were either missing or had been replaced with galvanized steel when my Dad bought the boat. Thanks to Bristol Bronze I was able to get *Ruddigore* back into spec. I also replaced the stained and split seats with some new lumberyard mahogany, finishing with a Min-Wax gel stain, CPES, and many coats of Epiphanes varnish.

My artistic wife, Amy, ran a few computer font samples to see how the name graphic could look. We decided on a traditional looking set of letters and she chalked a stencil onto the transom. Then she freehanded the gold name over the dark mahogany. With a white pinstripe surrounding each script letter, it looked great.

The only work I was not comfortable tackling myself was the sail making. I toyed with the idea of buying a sailcloth sewing machine and putting together a kit, but I knew I wouldn't have the patience for it so near the end of the project. I also knew from my racing experience that sails had a huge impact on the performance of the boat, so I wanted them right. For some reason I viewed sewing the sails kind of like putting up wallpaper in a house. I've built many houses as a carpenter but have come close to destroying one after trying to hang wallpaper. I was not going to put myself through that grief, so I called most of the big national sail-makers to get some prices. I also contacted a semi-local loft, Yacht Sailmakers of Oshkosh. I got a real kick out of the owner; he was an old school businessman. "Web site? Now why would I need a web site to make sails?" was his response to one of my questions. Yacht Sailmakers wouldn't even accept a credit card for the work; I paid the invoice with a check. I could not be happier with the

results. The sails were custom-made for my exact spar dimensions at a pretty reasonable price. They set perfectly.

That spring I also tried my luck with multi-state beauracracy. I needed to register this 70-plus-year-old boat in Wisconsin, but I had no real paperwork. I had a picture of the boat with some expired Michigan numbers, dating from the 1970s. I contacted both state authorities and eventually figured an angle to satisfy them. After many personal letters and some sweet talking on the phone, I actually received a new Wisconsin boat registration with the correct year and serial number. I paid a whole 12 cents in taxes. Given the $2 sale price; five percent went to the state, half a percent went to the county, and another half a percent was paid to our local Lambeau Field renovation project for the Green Bay Packers. I was happy to give one cent to the Lambeau project — it's the one and only tax I actually voted for!

Finally launch day came on June 29th, three years and three weeks after *Ruddigore* reentered my life. My wife organized a great gathering of family, friends, neighbors, and fellow sailors at Windjammers Sailing Club. The *Green Bay Press Gazette*, our local paper, actually showed up for the launch ceremony. I popped a bottle of champagne and we sipped bubbly from plastic glasses

Rigged and ready — Ruddigore's *appearance is faithful to the original Alden design.*

during my launch speech. Then it was three cheers and into the drink she went. The first words out of my Dad's mouth were, "hey, look…. it doesn't leak!" We waved goodbye to the crowd and my dad and I went for a short sail on Green Bay. Although I didn't know it at the time, my friend Rich Luxton videotaped the festivities — a wonderful gift to keep for posterity. Fellow sailor and friend Dan Wassenberg said it best when he said "a thing of beauty and a joy forever." It was truly a great day.

Needless to say, my original plan to replace the centerboard bedlogs and get sailing was a little optimistic. But after I decided to go whole hog, I didn't put a time constraint on the project. To anyone undertaking such a project, I highly recommend keeping a logbook as I did. I did this out of habit and continued to make notes about various stages of the work. The logbook has been rewarding to look back on, and was even helpful in writing this chapter.

My advice to someone restoring a wooden boat is — be patient! I am less patient than I am dedicated. The project repeatedly took longer than I planned, but I didn't let the work consume me. Little things like family and employment have their priorities. During the second summer of the restoration, I came very close to buying a Sunfish. I desperately needed to get out on the water quickly and cheaply. I knew at this point in the project that *Ruddigore* was not going to satisfy either need. I eventually gave up on my Ebay quest for a Sunfish because I knew it would distract me and ultimately delay the whole project. I kept every receipt for the restoration, but doubt I will ever add them up. You know you're in deep when you really don't bat an eye for a $700 cover to put on a $2 boat!

I currently keep *Ruddigore* at Windjammers Sailing Club on the west shore of Green Bay. The majority of my time has been spent day sailing and teaching my girls the basics of sailing. As they gain confidence I plan to participate in some

weekly Tuesday night racing. My crew is super light and my old wood boat seems to keep pretty good pace with the rest of the Tuesday night cruiser and racer fleet. About the only thing I have left to do is apply the registration numbers. I was hoping to avoid the ugly things but a conservation officer was nice enough to let me off with just a warning last summer. It would have been a pretty stiff fine. I guess he appreciated the fact that the boat was much older than he was.

I really enjoyed bringing *Ruddigore* back to life. Teaching my girls to sail on her, just like my Dad did with me, has been a rewarding experience. Katie and Morgan get a kick out of recreating moments from my bedtime reading books, *Swallows and Amazons*. The Amazon, a 15-foot daysailer in the story, is very much like *Ruddigore* and it is captained and crewed by two young girls. I hope to keep the boat in the family forever; so far so good, given my daughters' interest. I have countless crayon drawings of the green and cream hull hanging in my office. And there's usu-

Just as author Healey learned to sail aboard his boat as a boy, he taught his daughters to sail aboard Ruddigore.

ally at least one "Rembrandt" on the refrigerator during the summer months. I try and get my Dad out on *Ruddigore* every time he visits in the summer. I also bring her up to his house on Little Bay de Noc, Lake Michigan over the 4th of July. It's great being out on the water with such a different type of boat. Little Bay de Noc is a world renowned walleye fishery. When *Ruddigore* is out among the countless aluminum fishing boats, she really stands out.

This past summer I was out sailing *Ruddigore* with my Dad and my two daughters when Tim Sr. recited an old saying that we've joked about for years: "Ahh, I wonder what the poor people are doing right now?" My oldest daughter, who had never heard the saying before, gave us both a funny look and said, "Poor people, mmm? I thought this boat cost two bucks!"

BOAT SPECS

Designer	John G. Alden, Naval Architects
Design Number	346-B
Year Built	circa 1931
Length OA x LWL x Beam x Draft	14'8" x 12'8" x 5'10" x 8 1/2" (board up), 2'6" (board down)
Construction	Cedar Planks over oak frames, bronze fastened
Displacement	Approximately 425 lbs.
Rig	Marconi rig 125 sq. ft.
Engine	Minn Kota electric motor plus a paddle

TOOL LIST
- Random orbital sander
- Palm sander
- Belt sander
- Bent tang file
- Long board manual sander
- Siding type scraper
- Cabinet scraper
- Table saw
- Hand drill and hand saw
- Utility knife, regular blade and carpet blade
- Dremel tool
- Hacksaw blades
- Router
- Planer (borrowed)
- Typical hand tools — screwdrivers, hammer, pliers, wrenches, etc.

KEY MATERIALS LIST
- Smiths CPES
- Interlux — two-part primer, Brightside Paint, Interdeck
- West System Epoxy and various fillers
- Epiphanes varnish
- Buff-colored English Braids rigging line
- Bristol Bronze fittings
- Oak stock
- Mahogany and spruce
- Bronze screws, bolts, etc. (Jamestown Distributors)
- Sails — Yacht Sailmakers, Oshkosh, WI

About the Author: Tim Healey is a project manager for an engineering and design/build company. He specializes in industrial construction projects ranging from beverage packaging to distribution center material handling systems. He has a BS degree in Construction Management from Michigan State University. Boating has long been Tim's favorite hobby, whether sailing, fishing, water skiing, paddling, cruising, or racing. Tim has owned at least half a dozen boats, restored a couple, and built two kid's dinghies. Although partial to wooden sailboats, he and his family can be found bouncing around the bay in an old 13-foot Boston Whaler, a boat that, like *Ruddigore*, he grew up with.

4

A Lyman Sleeper

BY DAN SCHEE

It was with justification that company advertising used to claim Lyman boats as "America's favorites." In the years following World War II, the Sandusky, Ohio boat builder produced an appealing lineup ranging from swift and buoyant-looking outboard runabouts to the able, high-sided Sleeper that is the subject of this chapter. Produced in the thousands, Lymans shared an immediately distinctive appearance thanks to their lapstrake or "clinker" construction. When it comes to boats that leave lasting impressions, Lymans must rank near the top of the list. Author Dan Schee is among those who fell under a Lyman's spell at an early age and who, years later, realized his dream of owning one.

As a youngster growing up in Sandusky, I was treated regularly to the sight of a Lyman boat effortlessly gliding through the choppy waters of Lake Erie. All around the lake, Lymans were regarded as the cream of the crop thanks to their seaworthiness and value. Quite a few of my friends and my parents' friends owned one. I never turned down an offer to go out on one of those boats and doubtless it was this childhood experience that planted a dream of someday possessing a Lyman of my own. There were a lot of Lyman knockoffs being made at that time but the classic lines of the Lyman and its ability to handle rough water hooked me for life.

I married in 1969 and, because of military service and subsequent civilian job assignments, my family and I spent the next 25 years living away from Lake Erie. Finally, in 1993 I accepted a job transfer back to the Lake Erie area and the search for my very own Lyman began in earnest. By then Lyman had long since succumbed to makers of fiberglass boats. But my dream of Lyman ownership was alive and well. My hope was to find a boat that was structurally sound but would still fit within our budget, which my wife and I had estimated would permit a purchase price of no more than $3,000.

After nine more years of scanning For Sale ads and trader magazines, and stopping at every Lyman parked in a yard at the side of the road, I finally found her in June of 2002! I was driving home from work and chanced upon a 1964 Lyman 25' Sleeper with a For Sale sign taped to her bow.

The 25' Sleeper was one of the first Lyman

The start of it all — author Schee's Lyman looked reasonably sound and the engine fired right up during his initial inspection.

models that had been redesigned with increased bow flare for a drier ride. The stem itself had an increased rake and a flared stern replaced the original tumblehome or barrel-back design. It was a beamy boat that could sleep two adults in a V-berth. The stability imparted by the wide beam made the boat perfect for fishing; the overall size meant the Sleeper could easily handle the choppy conditions often found on Lake Erie. During my initial inspection in the owner's yard, I learned that a prior owner had covered the entire deck with fiberglass, and that the cracked varnish had

peeled off all the mahogany trim.

I arranged to return later that week for a sea trial. If the engine fired and the boat didn't sink, I expected to hand over the check. As it happened, the boat ran like a champ. This offset her cosmetic failings. Still, I had no way of guessing the true

The high-sided hull and spacious cockpit of Lyman's 25-footer are evident in these brochure photos.

nature of the adventure that was soon to start. As things worked out, within two days of my initial inspection the sale was complete.

My plan was to run the boat from the Portage River in Port Clinton to the Huron River close to where I live, and then return later to pick up the trailer. My wife had an uncle who lived on the Huron River and he had an empty boat house with a lift. This would be my boat's new home for the season. Uncle Dick and I showed up at the boat on Saturday and we cast off, headed down the Portage River, gassed up, and then headed out on Lake Erie bound for Huron about 28 nautical miles away. As we passed Cedar Point, the boat started to list noticeably to starboard and the bow began rising higher and higher. In fact, we were taking on so much water that some of Lake Erie was now visible above the floorboards in the stern. The boat's only bilge pump was in the bow so it was not going to help. Dick and I spent the rest of the trip trading turns bailing water and finally got the boat up in the slings in the boat house where we both stood staring at this sorry excuse for a Lyman. All Dick could do was shake his head and walk away.

STARTING OUT

Having never taken on a project like this before, I had initially planned to run the boat for the remainder of the season, compile a work list based on observations, and then prioritize the needed repairs. Now, however, I had my first priority and it was unexpected — keep the boat from sinking! I knew from looking over the boat in the owner's yard that all of the fir plywood hull planking was solid and in good shape. There wasn't a square foot of hull, inside or out, that wasn't poked and prodded with my ice pick to see if any rot was present. So, where was that water coming from?

I spent almost the entire next week lying on my back on a raft with the boat hanging in the slings above me. When I found a seam with what looked like questionable caulk, I dug it out and put in a new bead of 3M 5200. Three sea trials later I discovered that the boat only took on water when running at full or close to full throttle. Back on the raft I went. After further inspection, I finally discovered that a scarf joint in one of the bottom planks had been put in backwards. As the speed of the boat increased, the water would force its way hydraulically through the leading edge of the joint and into the bilge. The faster the boat went, the more water found its way through the joint. To remedy this, I fabricated a temporary stainless steel patch, sealed the joint with 3M 5200 adhesive caulk, and screwed the patch in place over the scarf joint.

For the remainder of the 2002 season, I ran the boat as often as I could and found no more major issues. The fellow from whom I bought the boat had told me that the 318-cubic-inch Chrysler Marine engine had just had a complete overhaul and it performed as advertised. I knew that no mechanical work to the engine was needed. In fact, I knew that Lyman did not power its boats with Chrysler Marine engines in 1964, so I had a pretty good idea that this was a replacement engine. Further, the engine was equipped with electronic ignition, so I knew that this replacement took place at some point in the late 1970s to early 1980s.

The rest of the boat, however, was not as promising as the engine. The wiring looked like a bucket of worms. Apparently, if a prior owner removed a device from the boat, he simply snipped the wire and left it lying in the bilge. There was no rhyme nor reason to the circuits, nor were there enough fuses to handle what today's boater would expect. I even found a ground wire that had cloth insulation on it, meaning it was even older than the boat as cloth insulation virtually disappeared with knob and tube wiring in homes.

Cosmetically, it became apparent that all mahogany parts needed serious attention. The varnish was cracked, blistered, and peeling away, leaving the wood exposed to the elements. The fiberglass on the deck had a non-skid surface and had been painted over. The result was multiple peeling layers of paint, ranging in color from white to aqua. The weather stripping seal around the windshield and side curtain glass was dried out and cracked beyond repair, and the aluminum extrusions designed to hold the glass in place no longer did so.

Armed with my work list, I now needed to find a place where I could do the work. I could not fit a 25-foot boat in my garage. I found some heated warehouse space in Sandusky where I could both store the boat and work on it. Everything that could be taken off the boat (windshield, seats, deck hatch, helm, engine cover, etc.) was removed and hauled into my basement shop. The rest of the work would need to be done on the boat in the warehouse.

The warehouse was about 10 miles from my home and, ultimately, this meant that I needed two basic sets of tools — one at the warehouse, the other at home. When time was available during the week I would work on parts in my basement in the evenings. On weekends I would travel to the warehouse and work on the boat there. My initial plan was to finish part of the work and get the boat usable for the 2003 season. Then, it would go back into the warehouse and I would complete the balance of the work prior to the 2004 season.

Removing the windshield and various interior components was a little bit harder than I had anticipated. Lyman, like most wooden boat builders of that time, used silicon bronze screws. Although the heads of these screws looked like the normal Phillips head, I discovered, after destroying every other screw head for the first day or two, that these heads actually had a Frearson or Reed & Prince design head. Such heads have a comparatively deep profile that results in a larger surface contact area with the

driver bit, and I was using a bit that didn't really fit. Once armed with the proper bit, screw removal became easier but there were still several stubborn ones that wouldn't budge and finally snapped off. In these cases, after removing the component, I gripped the remaining shank of the broken screw with a set of vise grips and twisted it out of the hole. To anyone undertaking a similar project, I would recommend a set of easy-out screw extractor bits.

I now recognized that I would not have enough of the original screws left to reinstall the various components. My solution was to use readily available stainless steel screws in places that were above the waterline but not visible and save the remaining silicon bronze screws for exposed areas. Prior to reinstallation, I cleaned the heads of the silicon bronze screws with a wire wheel to remove old varnish that had built up over the years. I then stored the screws in a series of coffee cans segregated by screw size.

The windshield and all the deck fittings were originally installed with a bedding compound. I soon discovered that old bedding compound can act like an adhesive with age. In order to remove the windshield, I had to make a handle for a hacksaw blade and, using a propane torch, heat the blade to cut through the old bedding compound while at the same time inserting wedges between the windshield and the deck to pry the windshield off.

The component restoration done in my basement shop was not, for the most part, terribly complicated. The vast majority of this work consisted of removing the old varnish with a chemical stripper, sanding, staining, and recoating each part.

To facilitate stripping, I made a simple work surface out of a set of saw horses with three 2 x 4s running lengthwise and 1 x 1s attached crosswise, spaced about 10 inches apart. The result looked similar to a trellis. During the stripping process, I simply drew the blade of the putty knife across one of the exposed 1 x 1s and the spent stripper varnish residue fell away to the floor. I adopted this method as it was faster than scraping the residue into an empty coffee can, and it allowed me to use both hands.

Unlike the projects done at home, work at the warehouse was anything but simple. The cosmetic appearance of the hull wasn't all that bad and, as such, had been rather low on the priority list. My initial plan was to simply scrape off the multiple layers of bottom paint, sand, prime, and apply a new coat of copper bronze bottom paint, leaving the lapstrakes repair for the 2003 season. At least that was the plan.

One of my first discoveries was that a prior owner had used what appeared to be an automotive two-part body filler in the seam between the lapstrakes on the hull and the stem. Because wooden boats can flex while underway, but automotive body filler doesn't, the filler cracked, allowing water to enter the hull. (My scarf joint patch stopped the massive water intrusion but, mysteriously, there was still always a lot of water in the bilge and the pump ran almost continuously.)

I found that the best way to remove the body filler was with a Dremel tool with a small cut-off wheel. The thickness of this cut-off wheel almost perfectly matched the desired width of the resulting seam. However, digging out the automotive

A previous owner's effort to caulk seams at the stem using body filler resulted in leaks. The author removed the body filler with a Dremel tool and cut-off wheel.

body filler meant that the top coat paint on the hull had to be feathered into the cleaned stem seam as the body filler extended well over the adjoining lapstrakes. So much for not disturbing the hull paint! The hull would now have to be faired out and repainted for the 2003 season.

My next surprise resulted in scrapping any idea of putting the boat in the water for the 2003 season. A prior owner had covered the entire deck with fiberglass mat which wrapped around the gunwale. In effect, this encapsulated the wooden rub rail that ran around the entire periphery of the boat. Using a Wagner heat gun and a three-in-one putty knife, I began to remove the fiberglass mat from the bow deck. When heated, the resins used in fiberglass lose their adhesive properties and the mat can be pried away from the wooden substrate. This was a tedious job but progressed rather nicely. The good news here was that the condition of the plywood sub-deck was excellent.

The gunwale was another story. Once the fiberglass was removed from the rub rail, the entire rail — made of white oak — crumbled and fell to the floor. A professional rub rail replacement was not an option for two reasons. The first was economic: there was simply no room in the budget for this type of cost, which I estimated might total upwards of $1,000. The second was that, even if I could afford a professional replacement, the boat was simply not capable of being transported over the road to a professional's shop. Too many interior components had been removed for refinishing.

While I was a reasonably experienced woodworker, I knew that fabricating a new rub rail would be a challenge. Not only did this rub rail have a radial curve that formed the bow, it also had a longitudinal upward curve or sweep. What's more, the inside surface of the rub rail had varying compound angles that mated with the bow flare on the hull. With literally no viable options, I decided to go ahead and try the replacement myself. A purist would have built a steam box and bent the rub rail to form the required compound curves. I thought about doing just that, but I couldn't figure out how to get the different mating angles on the inside of the rub rail prior to bending the part, or how to bend the part and then accurately cut the different angles.

I chose instead to replace the rub rail in segments. I first milled white oak stock to the proper thickness. I then cut a series of segments about 10 inches long with a different mating angle to the hull and left each one about a half-inch wider than the finished outside curve. Then, using a compound miter saw, I dry-fit each segment to the boat by clamping it to the plywood sub-deck and carving away the inside radius to fit. Once I was satisfied with the overall fit of each segment, I glued and doweled each segmented joint and screwed them to the hull first from the inside through each rib and then downward through the sub-deck. At this point, the outside curve was not yet established. To create this curve I used a hand-held jig saw and eyeballed the curve estab-

The Lyman's rotted rub rail was replaced with a new one composed of segments about 10" long. Each one was dry-fit so that its inner face fit tightly against the hull.

lished by the overhanging sub deck. I left about an extra 1/8 inch, which was then finished off using a belt sander. It was at about this stage of the project that the various tenants and employees in the warehouse started to remind me of my original intent for this boat: "Dan, it's only a fishing boat."

Replacing the rub rails on both sides of the boat took about six weeks, dashing any last hope of having the boat in the water for any part of the 2003 season. At that point, I combined the remaining work planned for the 2003 season with that planned for the 2004 season and then rearranged the individual tasks into a revised work plan. I was adept at using project management software at work, and I now regret not using it for this project. In the long run, it would have been very helpful, and would have made keeping track of the budget much easier.

In the meantime, work on refinishing the loose parts in

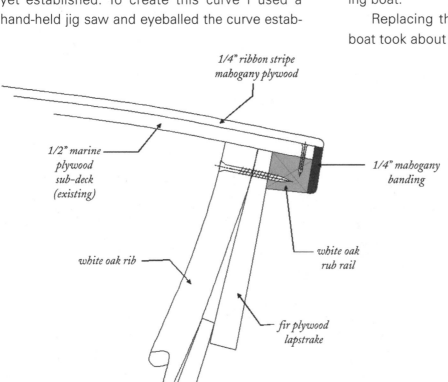

1/4" ribbon stripe mahogany plywood

1/2" marine plywood sub-deck (existing)

1/4" mahogany banding

white oak rib

white oak rub rail

fir plywood lapstrake

This sketch gives a good idea of the boat's construction. A varnished deck would later be installed atop the sub-deck.

In order to remove the fiberglass that had been applied to the boat's deck, it was first necessary to remove the king plank and toe rails.

my basement was progressing well. In order to remove the fiberglass from the deck of the boat, the boat's king plank and toe rails had to be removed from the bow deck. Both of these components, made by Lyman out of solid mahogany, were far gone and came off in pieces. The king plank runs down the centerline of the fore deck

from the windshield forward. The toe rails are about an inch thick and follow the curve of the bow on each side. Making a new king plank was relatively easy. I simply took the dimensions from the broken plank and made a new one out of new solid mahogany.

The toe rails were another matter. In the absence of a steam box, I chose to make new ones by laminating thin strips of mahogany. One of the two toe rails came off in two pieces. I simply aligned the two pieces of the rail together and traced the curve onto a piece of 3/4-inch plywood. Then I screwed clamp blocks to the plywood using the traced curve as a guide. Next I glued three strips of 1/4-inch mahogany and clamped them to the blocks. When the glue dried, the curve remained in the laminated strips. In order to avoid having to do this twice, I made the laminating strips twice as wide and then ripped the curved lamination down the center on a table

New toe rails were laminated out of thin strips of mahogany according to a pattern made from one of the old rails.

saw. The result was two mirror images, each with the same curve. Finishing operations required only rounding off the top two corners on each rail and using a block plane to taper the trailing ends down to about 1/2 inch. Once the rails were stained and finished, one would have to look very closely to see that they were not made from one piece of mahogany.

The only other major part that I ended up making in the shop was the bow hatch. The original hatch was made of 3/4-inch marine plywood with mahogany veneer on both sides. It had started to delaminate. The hatch itself is only about 20" x 20". I couldn't justify buying a whole 4' x 8' sheet of this very expensive plywood, so I ended up edge joining 3/4-inch solid mahogany boards into a blank about 22" x 22". I used the original hatch as a template, duplicating the outside shape and the hole for the glass (and a groove on the underside that held a foam seal) with a router using a flush cutting bit with bearing guide. I have to admit this effort took two tries as I got a bit too aggressive with the router and split the first attempt beyond repair. Finishing operations were to round over the top edge to allow water runoff, and to reinstall the glass and grill after the finish was applied.

One of the perceived downsides to wooden boat ownership is the amount of routine annual maintenance. Traditional spar varnish used on the

The original 3/4" plywood bow hatch was replaced with a new one made up of mahogany boards assembled to create a blank that was then shaped as necessary.

brightwork requires periodic sanding and top coating due to its tendency to yellow from the sun. Such maintenance can be protracted because a significant cure time between coats is needed. Because of this cure time I decided early on to use a urethane spar varnish instead of traditional spar varnish. This was more of a timeline decision than an economic or restoration decision. Quite simply, I could apply more coats of urethane in a shorter amount of time.

The basic steps for either traditional or urethane varnish remain the same: after the old varnish is removed, prepare the wooden surface by sanding. In some cases, bleaching the wood is required if there are any dark stains present. Then, apply the wood stain. Lyman used a very specific mahogany filler stain. Finding a match for the Lyman Mahogany Filler Stain # 4973 was easy because a paint store in Sandusky still stocks it. This stain comes out of the can with the approximate consistency of mayonnaise and needs to be thinned 50 percent prior to application. It is applied across the grain and then wiped down with the grain after it has had a chance to penetrate. I had an empty plastic jar that I used to thin the stain. Because it had a screw-on lid, it was easy to periodically shake the jar so that stain pigments did not settle, resulting in an uneven appearance.

Some people I had talked to had brushed the stain while others ragged it on. I found that a two- or three-inch foam brush to apply the stain, followed by a paper towel to wipe off the excess, worked well. I found that blue paper shop towels were better suited for this than household paper towels because they absorbed more material and did not leave little pieces of fiber behind. I also found that it was much easier to apply a second coat of stain if the initial result wasn't dark enough, rather than wiping off excess stain that was left to penetrate for too long. This particular stain fills and penetrates very quickly so it is better to apply and wipe away excess stain in small areas. Consistent pressure applied when wiping down the stain was the best way to ensure an even color and appearance.

I applied at least five finish coats of spar urethane, block sanding between each coat. When using traditional spar varnish, the final step would be to apply a sealer. Because I used urethane spar varnish, I thinned the urethane about 50 percent and used this as a sealer.

By now it was January of 2004 and the project was progressing more slowly than expected. I was ready to seek some help. One of the other warehouse tenants, from whom I was subletting my space, did automotive restoration and body work. Over a period of time, Monty and I had gotten to know each other quite well. Now, Monty was getting to a point in his work where he was going to need the space occupied by my boat. I had replaced the rub rails and had just about finished removing the rest of the fiberglass from the deck when Monty came up with an idea. Instead of me paying him rent for the space, why not hire him to fair out the hull and paint it while I finished off the new deck. I had seen Monty's meticulous work so I had no problem with this arrangement. The thought of actually finishing this project perked me up again, and getting back into the work kept me busy.

From the start of the project I had planned on putting down ribbon-stripe mahogany plywood for the new deck as this was one of the classic features of original Lymans. I now had a clean sub-deck and fully shaped rub rails so the next step was to install a mahogany fascia around the white oak rub rails. Because I wanted the deck to lie on top of the fascia, the fascia needed to be installed first. The final effect would suggest that the mahogany deck itself wrapped around the gunwale. I milled up the mahogany by ripping 3/4-inch solid mahogany into several two-inch strips about 10-feet long. In order to save material, I sawed the 3/4-inch strips down to 3/8-inch thickness and then finished them by running them

A clean, tight sub-deck formed the underpinnings for the ribbon-stripe mahogany foredeck that the author had planned on installing since the early days of the restoration project.

through a thickness planer until they were 1/4-inch by two-inches wide.

I began at the bow, soaking the center of one of the mahogany strips for several hours and then warming it with a heat gun to make it pliable enough to bend right around the bow. The fascia strips were attached using 3M 5200 adhesive caulk along with a few stainless steel finish nails intended to hold the banding in place until the adhesive cured. I installed the fascia flush with the bottom of the rub rail and let it stand proud of the sub-deck by about 1/4-inch. Once the adhesive set, I used a router and a block plane to get the top edge of the banding about 1/16-inch proud. This would ensure a tight seam with the edge of the plywood deck material.

Now it was time to move ahead with the decking. I established the centerline of the boat by locating the point of the bow and the midpoint of the stern, and then marking the line between with a chalk line. I next positioned the mahogany plywood with one factory edge set on the centerline of the boat, and clamped the sheet into place through the hole for the forward hatch. With the decking secured, I drew a pencil line around the perimeter using the completed rub rail as a guide. Then I unclamped the plywood, moved it to a sawhorse and cut away the excess material with a jig saw. leaving about 1/8-inch of extra material.

It should be noted that, because the beam of the boat exceeded eight feet, I had to use 5' x 10' sheets of plywood to avoid exposed seams. Doing so meant that I could match up the factory edges well enough to look good, and that I didn't have an exposed seam where water could potentially intrude and ruin the sub-deck. I did end up with a seam running down the center of the bow, but this would later be covered with the king plank, forward hatch, and windshield.

With the rough cut now complete on the new deck material, I applied a liberal amount of the 3M 5200 adhesive onto the sub-deck with a notched trowel and then repositioned the deck material back in place. This is where I learned that one never has enough clamps. In those areas where the deck would later be covered by the king plank and forward hatch, I attached the new deck material to the sub deck with stainless steel screws.

After the adhesive had set, I removed the clamps and finish trimmed the new deck plywood to the rub rail with a router set up with a flush-trim bit and guide bearing. I would later round over the

top edge of the new plywood deck and the bottom edge of the rub rail banding with a quarter-roundover bit also equipped with a guide bearing. The whole process was repeated for the starboard side of the bow, across the stern, and finally along both sides. Obviously, with 10-foot long plywood panels and a 25-foot long boat, there had to be exposed seams somewhere. I elected to place these seams along the sides of the boat as the length of each seam would be minimal and would be hidden to some extent by the side panels of the windshield. Wherever there was a seam, I made sure that I applied mahogany-colored bedding compound to help prevent water form working its way down to the sub-deck.

Finally, for each through-deck fitting (clam shell air vents, gas filler, etc.) I made a matching hole in the new deck using the existing hole in the sub-deck as a guide. I used the same straight-cutting router bit that I had used to final trim the deck to the rub rail banding. First, I drilled up from the bottom with a 5/8-inch spade bit and then inserted the router bit down from the top through the drilled hole. The result was that the guide bearing on the router bit followed the existing hole exactly and the hardware fit like a glove.

By now the boat had reached a point where it was ready for final sanding, staining, and finishing. The ribbon-stripe plywood panels used to cover the deck had a very smooth finish. However, before installing anything on the deck I first sanded the entire deck, beginning with 150-grit paper and then working my way down to 220-grit. I opted to use a palm-held random orbit sander. The absence of obstacles made this go very fast.

Each half of the new ribbon-stripe deck was installed using liberal quantities of 3M 5200 and many clamps.

Once I had stained the entire deck and rub rail banding, and had allowed it to dry overnight, it was time to install the king plank and toe rails. I attached these to the deck using stainless steel screws through predrilled holes. Each hole had a 3/8-inch deep by 1/2-inch diameter counter bore. The counter bore would be used to accept a 1/2-inch diameter plug, or bung, cut from solid mahogany. Once I had determined the proper position and alignment of the king plank and toe rails, I marked their perimeter location with blue painter's tape. I then applied mahogany bedding compound inside the taped-off area. Next, I placed the king plank and rub rails into the compound and screwed the parts to the deck with #6 stainless steel screws. Finally, I glued the mahogany plugs into each of the counter-bored holes and cut them almost flush with the top surface using a Japanese backsaw. I then sanded the top of the plugs flush with the top of the part, and touched up the stain that was removed by sanding.

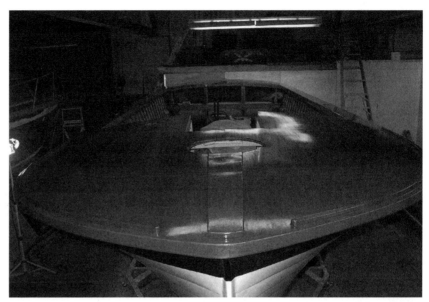

A new king plank covered the seam between the two halves of the deck. Here, the toe rails have been installed.

The project was now at the point where tangible, finished results could be seen on a daily basis. I applied a coat of thinned-down urethane as a sealer for the mahogany filler stain that I had applied to the new deck. The ribbon striped grain of the mahogany deck started to look terrific. I was now in the homestretch, or so I thought. It was the middle of July 2004 and the heat and humidity in the warehouse were pretty high. I discovered early in the process of applying urethane finish coats that it was virtually impossible to keep a wet edge. The urethane would start to tack up before I could complete one area and would not blend or flow into the next area of wet urethane. This required a lot of block sanding to remove the ridges left in the urethane.

At the recommendation of the paint store, I started using a commercial additive called Penetrol to extend the urethane's drying time. This additive retarded the cure time and allowed me to keep a wet edge on the urethane. I found that I got the best results by applying the urethane with a foam brush and sanding between each coat with 220-grit sandpaper. Six coats of spar urethane later, the deck was complete.

As I neared completion of the deck and rails, Monty was making progress on the hull. Lyman had attached hull planks with countersunk screws into the ribs. Clinch nails along the bottom edge of each strake joined the strake to the top edge of the adjacent one. As years pass, however, all of these fasteners can loosen up. They often require cosmetic treatment to hide the heads while smoothing out any wavy conditions that may have developed in the planking itself. It was now time to address these issues by fairing the hull.

My choice of materials here was, again, a timeline decision. Some, if not most, Lyman owners use a two-part epoxy combined with some type of filler to fair out a hull. The cure time with this material is often overnight. We opted to use

3M Marine Premium Filler. This is very similar to the automotive body filler that I had removed except that it doesn't dry as hard as the automotive type and will flex with the boat. It can be used both above and below the waterline.

Monty started out by going over the entire hull with an air file using 60-grit sandpaper. An air file is an air-driven sander that, unlike a random orbital finish sander, vibrates in a straight back and forth motion. The foot of the sander is also significantly longer than that of a finishing sander so it spans a larger area and results in a much flatter surface. First Monty removed all known high spots as well as sags in the existing paint, filled screw holes, etc. Then he inspected the hull for areas that were not sanded. These were the low spots. His experience in automotive body work no doubt helped him in truly differentiating one from the other. He filled the low spots with the marine filler and continued to work down the high spots with the air file. After he was satisfied that the hull surface was flat, he re-sanded the entire hull progressing up to 120-grit sand paper.

Once he was satisfied with the surface condition, Monty applied the first coat of primer. Next, he block sanded the coat of primer by hand with 180-grit paper. He then applied a second coat of primer and block sanded it with 220-grit paper. The hull was now ready for the top coat. Early on, I decided to paint the hull a traditional Lyman white with a red waterline stripe. Most Lyman owners also paint a contrasting color on the sheer strake next to the gunwale in order to accentuate the lines of the boat. I chose this accent color to be a high gloss black in order to coordinate with the light gray bimini top and the light gray cushions. Both had come with the boat and were in such good condition that I saw no reason to replace them. Much to Monty's cha-

grin, he knew that a high gloss black would magnify each and every imperfection and he would have to make absolutely certain that this plank was as smooth and flat as possible. Both the black sheer strake and the white hull took two coats of paint. Monty also used Penetrol with the top coat paint to retard the curing time and keep the wet edge longer. Between coats, we block sanded the entire hull with 220-grit sandpaper.

It should be noted here that extreme caution was used when sanding so as to preserve the line that was scribed into the hull for the waterline. Eradicating this line would require that the boat be launched and marked for how the boat sat in the water. This was a step I wished to avoid at all costs.

Below the waterline the work was a little harder simply because it was harder to access the surfaces. The boat was sitting in a cradle on a trailer about two feet off the floor. All the old layers of bottom paint had to be removed by scraping, and the planking seams needed to have the old caulk removed and replaced. Little by little we whittled away at this while we were waiting for something

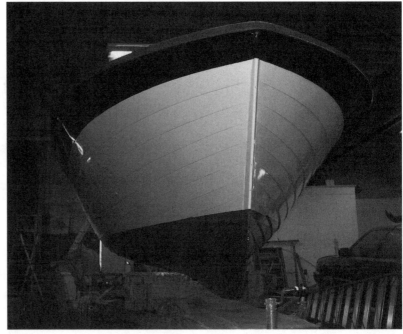

Much fairing, filling, and sanding provided a base for the boat's beautiful paint job: white hull, black sheer strake, and a red boot-top stripe.

else to dry or set up. Both Monty and I kept putting this part of the project off because of the physical difficulty of getting to the surfaces involved, but eventually it was the only thing left to do. The main focus was to remove all of the old caulk, then re-caulk each seam with the 3M 5200, fill the screw countersinks with 3M Marine Premium Filler, prime the entire surface with a red lead primer, and then finally apply two coats of copper bronze bottom paint. After this was completed, the boat was ready to have the windshield, deck fittings, and interior installed.

Prior owners had neglected the condition of the boat's bilge. Although all of the wood was sound, the bilge was filthy. It needed a thorough cleaning and a fresh coat of paint before I could route any of the new electrical wiring. A stiff wire brush and an array of plastic scrapers and a shop vac removed all of the debris that had accumulated. I also found that a small, narrow, flexible Japanese backsaw worked well to get into the voids between the ribs and the inside of the lap-strakes. It was important for these voids to be opened so that water in the bilge could flow forward to the bilge pump in the bow.

It was now time to begin to reinstall all of the components that had been removed and transported to my shop. I elected first to rewire the boat as there was easy access to all areas where the wiring needed to be routed. Fortunately, when I removed the helm I numbered all of the terminals on the switches and gauges before removing any of the wires. As I installed the electrical components, I simply matched up the numbers on the terminals with the appropriate wire coming into the helm from the device. I also chose to use a bus bar panel setup that I had seen in a friend's identical Lyman. I purchased *The 12 Volt Bible for Boats* at a local marine store. This book covers marine electrical systems and I wanted to be sure that I was rewiring the boat in a safe manner. I opted to purchase all of the wire and heat shrink connectors at a marine outfitter to ensure safe operation of the electrical system.

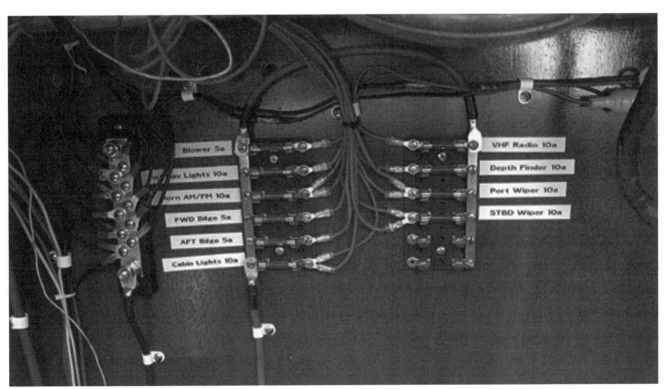

The boat was completely rewired and all fuses were clearly labeled.

I also chose to install a Jabsco compact manual head with a six-gallon holding tank in the cuddy cabin. It only required two through-hull fittings and one pump-out fitting in the deck. I must admit, it was rather painful to drill a hole in the brand new completed mahogany deck.

The remaining components were now installed in the reverse order to which they were removed. Before I knew it, the boat was ready to be launched. On our way to the marina, I stopped after a mile or two and checked the tie-down straps to make sure they hadn't loosened up. I did this in the parking lot of what was once the Lyman Boat Works, and took the opportunity to snap a picture of the restored boat in front of the site where it was first built. This complex is now a marina and entertainment complex named "Lyman Harbor."

The actual launch was uneventful. My marina had made plans to allow me to leave the boat in the launch slings over the weekend to allow the wood to swell. After only 45 minutes, the packing seals had tightened up and there was no water entering the bilge, so I cast off and took her to the slip. I spent the next two weeks finishing up odds and ends that hadn't been needed prior to launch. Then I took her to the Lyman Boat Owners Association (LBOA) "All Wooden Boat Show." It was at this show that an LBOA official asked if I would be willing to take the boat out on Lake Erie the next day for a photo shoot. I am happy to report that a photo of my boat, *My Viagra*, was selected to be in the LBOA 2005 calendar. In July of 2005, the boat was judged Best of Show at the Lyman Regatta, an event judged by ex-employees of the company.

I primarily use the boat for fishing, and take occasional cruises out on the lake to the islands or to a dockside restaurant for dinner. The running joke among my dock mates is that I have to vacuum out the bilge instead of pumping it out. The second bilge pump I added in the stern has never, to my knowledge, come on. For the 2005 season,

the only task I had was to apply a fresh coat of bottom paint. The spar urethane used on the deck is still pristine thanks, in part, to a full mooring cover I had made for the boat. The hull still looks as if it were made out of fiberglass.

Eventually I would like to add a bow rail to the boat. I already know that a transom replacement will be needed sometime down the road. (When refinishing the transom that is currently in the boat, I sanded through the veneer in a couple of spots, effectively limiting its life.) And that temporary patch I put on the backwards scarf joint two years ago? It's still there and probably will remain there until one or both of the planks need to be replaced.

IN RETROSPECT

In calendar months, the total project took three months shy of two years to complete. Obviously, I did not or could not spend every available spare minute working on this project. The untimely deaths of both my mother and my wife along with the demands of my job in the automotive supplier industry took priority over restoring an old wooden boat. The project was both frustrating and euphoric at the same time. Probably the most rewarding part of the project was finding a way to fix the job stopper — the rotted out rub rail.

Lyman owners, such as myself, are very fortunate to have a number of internet web sites devoted to the preservation of these boats. Each of these sites has extensive Q&A sections where people just like me can ask a question and, within a day or so (sometimes hours), get an answer from either an expert or another owner who has gone through the same ordeal. This, plus the direct contact with other Lyman owners in my area, proved to be the most valuable assets I could have hoped for.

I paid $2,500 for the boat in June of 2002 and estimate that I spent close to another $7,000 in materials and parts over the course of the project. That places my total investment right around

No wonder Lymans are popular! The time and effort invested in the restoration of this able 25-footer produced an outstanding result that is evident to all, and the boat's market value today far exceeds her owner's cash outlay.

$9,500. What is the boat worth today? It's only worth what someone is willing to pay for it, but certainly I could expect something over $25,000 in my local area. I've been told that if this boat were offered for sale in New England or upstate New York it could command a much higher price.

Buying and restoring an old wooden boat is a wonderful experience. Before you decide to take the leap, make sure you know exactly what your expectations are for the complete project. Restoring an old wooden boat is not unlike automotive restoration. If you want a concours quality "trailer queen," plan on spending a lot of time and money on each and every detail. If you want a "driver", as was my case, and you simply want the vessel to be seaworthy, safe, and look decent,

there are shortcuts you can take. Just don't shortcut on materials. There are very good reasons to use only marine plywood, coatings, sealers and, most importantly, engine components. The ribbon-stripe mahogany marine plywood I used came from a local supplier and I believe he purchased it from a company named World Panel. Lastly, have the boat surveyed by a professional. I was lucky and did not run into anything (other than the rotted rub rail) that would not have been found in a marine survey.

I've been asked if I would I do it again. Let's just say that I recently spotted a 16-foot Lyman outboard with a For Sale sign on the bow. I'm trying to find reasons not to go ahead and buy it. Looks like all it needs is a paint job . . .

BOAT SPECS

Brand	Lyman
Model	Soft Top Sleeper*
Hull ID	#K1331
Year Built	1964
Designer	Anthony Giovagnoli
Length x Beam x Draft	25'1" x 8'10" x 2'4"
Construction	Fir plywood over oak frames
Displacement	3,500 lbs.
Engine	Chrysler 318 (225 hp)
Advertised Speed	30-35 mph (now 25 mph)
Prop	3 Blade 14" x 12"
Original List Price	Approx. $5,200 base
Purchase Price 2002	$2,500

*Although the boat is currently configured as a soft top, the factory hull records show the boat was originally built as a hardtop and had been converted by a prior owner.

TOOL LIST

Stationary Power Tools
- 10" rigid table saw
- 13" rigid thickness planer
- 8" Craftsman joiner
- 12" Craftsman band saw
- Dremel tool with cutoff wheel
- Ryobi sanding center
- 10" Craftsman miter saw
- Delta dust collection system
- 42" Delta wood lathe
- 6" bench grinder

Portable Power Tools
- 19.2V Craftsman cordless drill
- 19.2V Craftsman cordless trim saw
- Craftsman 3" belt sander
- 3/8 " Chuck Skil drill
- 19.2V Craftsman cordless reciprocating saw
- 1/4" Black & Decker jig saw
- 1 1/2 hp Craftsman router
- 6" DeWalt palm sander
- 2 hp Craftsman plunge router
- Wagner heat gun
- 7" Skil circular saw

Miscellaneous Hand Tools
- Frearson head screwdrivers
- Crescent wrenches
- Various scrapers and putty knives
- Open and box end wrenches
- Block planes
- Various pliers
- 14" – 36" quick-release clamps
- Wire crimping tool
- Spring clamps
- Continuity tester
- Sanding blocks
- Japanese backsaw
- Coping saw
- Notched trowels
- EZ-out screw extractors
- Box knife
- 1/4 - 1" inch chisel set
- Hand miter saw
- Finishing and claw hammers
- Vise grips
- Wedges
- Scratch awl
- Propane torch

About the Author: Dan Schee's family moved to the Sandusky, Ohio area in 1952, four years after Dan's birth. Dan grew up boating on Lake Erie where he learned how to water ski behind a 1950s vintage 18-foot Lyman Islander. In fact, boating runs in the family. Dan has extensive woodworking experience thanks mostly to home improvement projects and, on a few occasions, he's built some small furniture pieces. The Lyman was his first boat project. In 2004, Dan retired from the automotive supplier industry after 30 years, but went back to work as a quality engineer when he missed the daily challenges and the interaction with people. He says he will keep at it as long as work doesn't cut too deeply into his fishing time.

5

A Chris-Craft Kit Boat

BY CHUCK NAGY

America's post-World War II boating boom offered something for everyone. Hundreds of companies emerged to produce "maintenance-free" fiberglass and aluminum boats. Well-established builders who stuck to wood construction did so at their peril. Slow to accept change, Chris-Craft sought new ways to market its wooden boats. Among Chris-Craft's more successful ideas was the introduction in 1950 of its boat kits for the do-it-yourself builder. "Buy a Chris-Craft Kit and SAVE!" read the ads. The kits included rowboats, runabouts, a 21-foot Express Cruiser, and a popular little eight-foot pram that sold for $49. "Own a new CHRIS-CRAFT for as little as $49 full price!" The kits promptly became fast sellers and one of those little prams survived to become the object of affection described in this chapter.

Over the years, my wife Nancy and I have traveled the Blue Star Highway many times. The road runs along Lake Michigan between South Haven and Saugatuck, Michigan and it is always a beautiful drive. Besides the scenery, we enjoy the roadside restaurants, exploring the surrounding area, and shopping. Over the years we've learned that behind one of our favorite antique shops we can usually count on seeing some rather unusual items. One day in August, 2002 a curious-looking, eight-foot, aqua-colored wooden boat caught my wife's eye.

The little orphan boat was sitting on the grass. My first thought was that it was from an old children's amusement park ride where the boats go round and round in a big water tank. On the other hand, the outboard motor controls indicated that is was indeed a real boat. As we mused over the little craft, we both thought it would make a fun boat to use on the Black River at South Haven where we have a summer place. When it's rough and windy on Lake Michigan, the big boats remain in their slips and the river is plied by all manner of dinghies, inflatables, and other small craft.

Because I had never owned a boat, I wanted a friend with experience to look at it. He not only gave the boat two thumbs up, he also offered to haul it back to South Haven! The antique dealer wanted $375, but after some negotiation we

This photograph shows author Nagy's little boat just as she looked on the day he spotted her behind a favorite antique store.

struck a deal for $350. With retirement nearing, the restoration of the boat sounded like a perfect project and so, seemingly from out of the blue, "messing about in boats" became my new hobby. Little did I know that boat restoration would grow to become a passion.

Once the boat was home, I did a more thorough survey. The antique shop owner had very little information or history on the vessel and, despite my friend's positive comments, I had no idea what I was looking at. Fortunately the boat, built principally out of marine plywood, was structurally sound. Most of the needed work appeared to be cosmetic. It was, in fact, a perfect boat for a first-time restorer. Before I began the actual work, I realized that record keeping would be important. In my case, this involved taking pictures, labeling parts as they were removed, mak-

ing measurements and drawings, and keeping track of items to be purchased. Photos can greatly aid in boat restoration. I did not have a digital camera for this restoration so I took only a minimal number of photos. I wish I had taken more.

The boat's diminutive size meant it fit easily into the garage. Our two-car garage became the boat shop. Here I was able to work most winter days with only a kerosene heater, although I subsequently installed a 35,000 BTU gas wall heater. Before starting work on the boat, I partitioned off the back five feet of the garage to make a room for a small workbench, a vice, and a tool storage area. Limited space and limited funds dictated the number and type of tools I could have. My power tools included a small table saw, skill saw, jig saw, electric drill, palm sander, belt sander, and a bench grinder. It's worth noting that today, thanks to comparatively inexpensive tools available in home improvement stores, it's easier to expand one's arsenal than in the past. My experience with these tools has been good. Many come with lifetime warranties. Watching for sales, I have purchased power drills, sanders, and jig saws for as little as $10 and $20. At those prices they become throwaway items, even without warranties. I also had the basic hand tools, in addition to a lifetime collection of screws, nuts, and bolts, all of which saved many trips to the hardware store.

There was no dry rot in the boat. The only structural problem appeared to be a weak transom whose inboard side was also scratched and rough. Clearly the transom needed to be repaired or replaced. After considering many alternatives I decided to add a 3/4-inch piece of solid mahogany on the inside of the transom, which would both reinforce it and cover the existing cosmetic problems. I purchased a mahogany board from our local Menards home improvement store. Granted this was not marine-grade lumber but I knew the boat would be trailered and not left in the water for more than a day at a time. Using the transom side rails as a guide, I created a template of cardboard. I used the template to trace the pattern on the mahogany, and cut out the new piece using my table saw.

A trial fitting showed the new transom board would fit nicely, although the stern corner braces were now too long. I was able to shorten them by cutting them back 3/4" with a small hand saw to allow for the now thicker stern. Before installing the transom, I faired its edges for the tightest possible fit. (Fairing is a great little nautical term that gives boat builders latitude to make corrections in

The pram's simple marine plywood structure is evident in this photograph. A new inner transom was one of the few structural upgrades that the boat needed.

A 3/4" mahogany board was installed with epoxy and screws to strengthen the original plywood transom.

their work!) I then used West System epoxy and screws with finish washers to secure the new piece to the inside face of the original transom.

With the transom repair complete, I knew that I had to protect the top of the joint against water intrusion between the two sandwiched pieces. To cover the joint, I attached a 1 1/2-inch piece of mahogany horizontal indoor trim, again from Menards. This finishing strip was bedded in epoxy and screwed to the mahogany portion of the transom. Rather than countersinking and plugging the new screw heads, I used brass screws and brass finish washers. This was easy and I liked the look so well that I did it on most of the trim. It was a great way to get a little brass on the boat.

Coming up with a repair plan for the foredeck

was the next task. The old deck was composed of two pieces of plywood with a joint in the middle. After stripping the old deck of its paint, I tried staining the plywood but was not happy with the results. Stumped for ideas I made a 50-mile trip to Johnson's Lumber in Charlotte, Michigan to look at marine lumber. The counter people were eager to help a novice like me. We found a 4' x 4' sheet of okoume ribbon mahogany plywood for $18 that I thought would look great on the deck. Back in the shop I used the old deck as a template and transferred the pattern to the okoume. Next, using a saber saw, I cut a piece to cover the entire deck. Using various clamps, temporary nails, and contact cement, I laminated the new piece to the old deck. This was an easy fix and the resulting deck is now a real eye catcher.

A key modification made to the original boat by a previous owner was the installation of decking. The author replaced the original deck with a new one made of okoume plywood.

I applied several coats of Pettit Captain's varnish. In so doing I covered, to some degree, my misadventures with a belt sander. I had used the belt sander to speed up the deck sanding. Unfortunately I had burned through a layer of the okoume at the port edge of the deck. Replacing the deck would have meant another trip to Charlotte and several hours of labor. I decided I would have to live with it. The mistake reminded me that when you buy a new car, you worry about getting the first scratch. You know that sooner or later it will happen. When it does happen it is almost a relief. Now that the pressure was off, I realized this boat would never be perfect. "Close enough" became my new mantra. Coming to grips with the level of quality one can accept is very liberating. I believe that if your skill level comes close to your quality expectations, the project will be enjoyable. If not, frustration is the likely result.

In retrospect, it would have been much easier to repaint the boat that cute aqua that Nancy liked so well. However, almost from the start of the project I could picture in my mind's eye the dramatic look of a varnished interior. Stripping the interior of its existing finish proved to be, without a doubt, the most difficult part of the restoration. I did not keep track of the total number of hours spent on this stage of project but I can say that it was tedious, difficult, frustrating, and time-consuming. If the paint had been oil-based, it might have been easier to remove. Unfortunately, it was probably a water-based paint applied over previously unprotected wood. The result was that the paint penetrated so deeply that even today, if you look closely, some of the aqua color is still visible beneath the varnish.

During the paint removal process, I tried strong chemical strippers, citrus strippers, heat guns, and pressure washers all with mixed results. Dad's paint stripper from Wal-Mart, seemed to be the most effective, yet getting the paint out of the cracks and deep down in the grain was almost impossible. I tried every tool in my toolbox, then went out and bought more tools, looking for that one magical tool that would do the trick. There wasn't one. The stripping process involved using a combination of tools: awls, nails, dental picks, steel toothbrushes, wheel brushes, sanding wheels, and numerous scrapers. I picked and scraped away until the stripping was completed. Finally, when it was done, I had a better understanding of why I spent so much time getting down to bare wood – I'm fascinated by the feel, smell, and beauty of wood.

It was at this point that I decided I would need help to achieve the results I wanted. I understood that the boat's final appearance would depend largely on surface preparation, the grunt work of restoration. Yet, even after the hours spent stripping the boat's interior of paint, I did not feel that I possessed the patience or knowledge to do the preparation correctly. As it happened Ron, my friend and neighbor, had plenty of boat restoration experience that included a variety of 16- to 23-foot runabouts and cruisers. Ron's approach to such work is very precise and fussy, as compared to my close-enough attitude. As things developed, we found that we worked very well together, compromising as necessary and having a great time.

Most of the preparation work involved sanding with a palm sander and finish sanding by hand. When sanding, we used 3M sandpaper — first medium and then fine — discarding sheets as soon as they became clogged. Removal of the paint on the hull was not necessary as much of it was solidly adhered and would make a good surface for the final finish. Instead, we feathered the paint edges and filled surface imperfections with Pettit's 7191 Mender, great for filling screw heads, scratches, low spots etc. Lightly applied with a putty knife, Mender can be sanded in one to two hours.

With the surface prepared, we vacuumed the hull and went over it with tack cloths before applying the primer coat. I chose Pettit's 6149 Undercoater. It is not recommended under the waterline if the boat is to be in the water more than two days in a row, but this was not a consideration in my case. The boat would live on its trailer between its waterborne adventures. I applied the primer as carefully as a finish coat because, as Ron pointed out, primer brush strokes will sometimes show through.

The first painter applied the finish coat of Pettit's Easy Poxy 3175 High Gloss White with a roller. The second painter followed close behind with a high quality brush, keeping a wet edge and leveling (tipping) the stipples caused by the roller. This method imparted such a smooth finish that the boat looked like it had been spray painted.

Finishing the boat's exterior mahogany deck and trim involved entirely different methods and materials. I used Gloucester 711A Mahogany Wood Filler to fill, seal, and color the mahogany before varnishing. The filler was first thinned with paint thinner to a paint-like consistency. We wiped the filler into the grain with a soft cloth. After 30 minutes, we wiped with the grain to achieve the desired shade. After that, we let the filler dry over night before smoothing all surfaces with fine-grade steel wool.

Finally, the time came to varnish the trim and interior. Although it initially seemed like I'd never need so much, I purchased a gallon of Pettit's Z-Spar 1015 Captain's Varnish. After I started varnishing, it became clear that my little boat would require more material than I'd guessed to get the desired finish. Because varnish is cheaper by the gallon, I was glad I hadn't planned to do the job with a couple of quarts.

Varnishing tips:
- Pour only the amount needed for the job because the slightest amount of dust or dirt will contaminate varnish; pour the balance into clean one-quart cans.
- Do not stir varnish.
- Use a high quality black china bristle Conona brush for the first coat, and a throw away foam brush for the finish coats.
- Keep a good wet edge and try to avoid going back over your work.
- Use a fine sandpaper to flatten the gloss between each coat, being careful to vacuum and go over the surface each time with clean tack cloths.

I'd read enough to know that several thin coats work better than thicker coats as the chance of runs is much reduced. After I applied several

Here is No Wake *in all her painted and varnished glory.*

coats I felt the finish had the look I wanted, and it was thick enough to offer protection against minor dings.

Towards the end of the restoration I began to shop for a motor that would be appropriate for the boat, something from the 1950s. I found a 1953 5 1/2-hp Johnson Challenger from Van's Marine in Grand Rapids Michigan. Van's has a huge inventory of modern and antique rebuilt motors and parts, looking a lot like an outboard motor museum.

The outboard required some modification by Van's in order to connect the motor to the existing Evinrude controls. Since neither Ron nor I had seen how the previous motor had been hooked up, we spent a lot of time sorting it out. Correctly wrapping the steering cables around the steering column was an adventure. In one configuration we would turn the wheel right and the motor would turn left. When we tried again the motor would not turn at all. Eventually the motor was hooked up correctly. The motor ran well on the maiden voyage, but the boat would not plane. I concluded it might plane if operated by an 80-pound boy or if it had a more powerful motor. The chances of me getting down to that weight were pretty slim so I needed more power.

It was shortly after I purchased the Johnson outboard that I became ever more curious about the boat's origin. There was continuing speculation from Ron and others that this was a Chris-Craft kit boat. During the project, I had found several boat pieces stamped with what appeared to be part numbers. This suggested that whoever

This original factory photograph shows Chris-Craft's Pram kit together with a finished boat. (Courtesy Mariner's Museum)

had produced the boat was some sort of "real" company. My curiosity took me to the library. There, I found the book *Chris-Craft* by Jack Savage, which included a section called "Chris-Craft in a Box." This was the confirmation I was looking for.

Chris-Craft sales literature showed the original pram kit did not have a deck, steering wheel, or outboard motor controls so my boat had clearly been modified. Additional research, searching the internet, and conversations with boat aficionados

told me that we really had something different. My first thought was, "If I had known this earlier I would have done a better job." However, I knew that had I attempted a perfect restoration the boat probably would still be unfinished.

A couple of years later at a South Haven, Michigan boat show I had a chance to meet and chat with Chris Smith, namesake and nephew of the founder of Chris-Craft. He related that Chris-Craft kit boats owed their existence to the fact that so much scrap wood was going to waste in the factories. The kit boats seemed a great way to solve the problem. In fact, demand grew so rapidly that the company had to purchase additional wood to meet it. Ads in magazines like *Boys' Life* created enough interest that, even several years after production ceased in 1958, the company still received orders for its kits.

My research also introduced me to the outboard motors that Chris-Craft had built until Mercury brought suit for patent infringement, causing Chris-Craft to cease outboard production in 1953. Today those outboards are hard to find and somewhat pricey. Several times I had come close to purchasing one, but they were either too rough or overly expensive. Then one day a friend called to say he had spotted a Chris-Craft outboard in an antique store. It was exactly what I wanted and reasonably priced at $300. I purchased it for $275 after spirited negotiation.

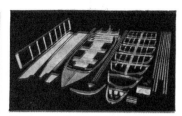

The range of Chris-Craft's boat kits is evident in this ad. The kits became popular and sold well to do-it-yourselfers who lacked the budget to purchase a factory-built boat.

I knew that the correct Chris-Craft kit boat decals would be very important for the boat's authentic appearance. Finding a source for the decals involved further digging for information and networking. While showing the boat at an Antique Outboard swap meet at The Michigan Maritime Museum in South Haven (sponsored by the Wolverine Chapter of Antique Outboard Motor Club; see www.aomci.org), I talked with several outboard motor restorers. From them I obtained the email address of George Burgess who duplicates outboard motor decals. For $10, George sent me the decals along with placement instructions. The Chris-Craft kit boat decals, along with the 1953 Chris-Craft 5 1/2-hp motor, make the boat correct to its heritage.

In the spring of 2003 I was finally ready to launch the boat that I had decided to name *No Wake*. The boat is light — about 200 pounds with motor — and I had purchased a 40" x 8' platform utility trailer for $200 for hauling and storing. Ratcheted tie-downs secure the boat to the carpeted bunks I built to fit the keel and stern, allowing the boat to slide easily into the water. The trailer has a short wheelbase, 12-inch tires, and slipper springs which make for a bumpy trailer ride and tricky back ups. Further trailer modifications may be necessary for longer trips.

I hoped to do the maiden voyage quietly so I could practice simply launching the pram, starting the engine, and checking out the little vessel's performance. Of course, the word got out and friends and family showed up at the ramp on the great day. Thankfully all went well; the motor started without a problem and, as this is basically a two-person craft, a succession of rides were given. Those on the dock later said that all they could see from behind were heads and shoulders

Tiny boats are easily transported on inexpensive utility trailers like this one.

and no boat. I found that the boat's handling is touchy. The boat turns very quickly because of its short length, and it is a bit "tippy."

Wherever my little Chris-Craft goes, it creates excitement and interest as people seem captivated by its looks and history. I find it amusing when young ladies ask for rides while young men with cigarette boats sit and scratch their heads. In fact, the boat has had an effect beyond anything I might have imagined. When *No Wake* appeared in *WoodenBoat* (issue #183, March/April 2005), I was amazed with all the email responses I received. To anyone thinking about a similar project, I would advise that you go for it. Do not let yourself think you might be getting in above your abilities. Instead, remember you are doing this for your own enjoyment. Most often you will find that your skill rises above those perceived "abilities." That's when boat restoration really becomes fun!

No Wake has led to my friendship with Mike Keifer, a highly skilled boat builder who owns Great Lakes Boat Building Company in South Haven. After seeing the boat, Mike offered me a couple days work each week during the summer of 2004. It was a dream job! With only a basic woodworking background I had a great deal to learn but Mike was very patient.

Little did I know that the lessons learned from Mike would soon come in handy. But they did. The first time I displayed *No Wake* at a show, one of the curious spectators informed me that he had both a Chris-Craft kit boat of his own and a 1950s Thompson Sea Skiff. Regarding the latter, he told me that he doubted he would have the time or energy to conduct a full-scale restoration. Several months later my newfound friend called to offer me the Sea Skiff. So, my first restoration project led to a second. Thus does my little kit boat continue to pay dividends.

BOAT SPECS

Brand	Chris-Craft
Model	Pram Kit Boat
Year Built	Unknown (circa mid-1950's)
Length x Beam x Draft	8' x 3'9" x 1'7"
Construction	Marine fir plywood over philippine mahogany frames, brass screws
Weight	200 lbs.
Engine	Chris-Craft 5 1/2-hp outboard
Original List Price	$49
Purchase Price 2002	$350

About the Author: Chuck Nagy is a 66-year-old native of Kalamazoo, Michigan and a summer resident of South Haven, Michigan. A United States Air Force veteran, he attended Kalamazoo Valley Community College. Chuck's working life has been varied. After seven years in vending machine sales, he was hired by the Michigan Commission for the Blind to develop, administer, and train the blind in the operation of vending concessions across the state. Chuck also designed, patented, manufactured, and sold wooden toys across the country. He also owned several businesses before he retired in 2003. Today, Chuck is active as a community volunteer, as a longtime member of the Kalamazoo Antique Automobile Restorers Club, and of course, with wooden boats.

6

A Sleek Sloop

BY STEVE KAPHAEM

Before fiberglass boats came to dominate the market, a rich variety of new wooden boats from a wide variety of designers filled the pages of boating magazines. Almost always, the boats were created to meet the requirements of one individual with the hope that others might also be interested in purchasing plans. Sometimes, however, a design was created with series production in mind. The sailboat that is the subject of this chapter was one of those. The Junior Holiday was created by the gifted Dutch designer Ericus Gerhardus van de Stadt (1910 – 1999) in 1953 as Design #41. The design was commissioned by Holiday Yachts, an American company with representatives in Long Island, Chicago, Pompano Beach, and Marblehead, Massachusetts. E. G. van de Stadt pioneered wing-section fin keels and balanced spade rudders. The Junior Holiday proved to be a well balanced little yacht of exceptional sailing ability. E. G. van de Stadt is credited with over 400 yacht designs and, at the time of his death in September 1999, it was estimated that some 25,000 boats of his design were delighting their owners throughout the world.

The ad was simple and straightforward: "For Sale: 25' Wooden Sailboat, $2500.00 call ... " It's a wonder to me now how a chance glimpse at a small local advertising circular could cause such a shift in my priorities over the next year or so. Almost without thinking, I dialed the number and arranged with the owner to see the boat. Wooden sailboats in this area of northern Michigan aren't rare, but they certainly aren't common. How could I not at least look? It was no great effort as the boat was located in Traverse City, only 15 miles away. One half hour later, my wife Marie and I

approached the address. The boat was easy to spot — an amorphous lump under a great collection of blue plastic tarps. Good news, for at least she was under cover. After introductions, the owner filled us in on what he knew about the boat's history.

Designed in 1956 by E. G. van de Stadt and built by the C. N. Vader yard in Holland, she was known in the U.S. as a Junior Holiday after the name of the importer, Holiday Yachts. She had been in fresh water all of her life, which can be good in some ways but not so good in others. We

Ads like this one from a 1956 issue of The Rudder *announced the presence of Holiday Yachts and the Junior Holiday sloop, one of which would survive to become the subject of this chapter.*

together and glued instead of the more usual method of grooved seams sealed with cotton caulking. Frames were one-inch-square, steam-bent oak. With a moderate draft of four feet, iron ballasted fin keel, and balanced spade rudder, the boat reflected quintessential Scandinavian design of the 1950s. She was named *Sante*, which is a French word meaning cheers.

I rapped on the hull in areas that normally can present problems in older wooden boats. These included the sections around the chain plates, the transom, and the stem. Wood makes many different sounds when struck with, say, the butt of a screwdriver. Hard ringing sounds are usually the sign of healthy wood; dull sounds that don't resonate might indicate deteriorated wood, as in rotted wood. The problem is that there are a whole range of sounds in between and some of these can be quite ambiguous. Plywood is one example where the outermost plies can be perfectly sound, disguising a mushy mess inside. If I am in doubt, I sometimes drill a small diameter hole straight through to examine the drill leavings, plugging the hole later with a wood bung or epoxy. In *Sante's* case, all the suspect areas rewarded me with a satisfying bang.

In due course we propped a ladder against the hull's side and went up for a look at the deck and cabin. Once aboard, we were greeted by a lot more peeling paint and varnish. We also found a nice mix of dry leaves, odd bits of wood, plastic soda bottles, and all the other indiscriminate detritus that somehow finds its way into a boat that has been out of the water for three years. Still, there was good news here — no water in the bilge and no dank smell of rotting wood. That doesn't mean rot isn't there, just that little mois-

unwrapped her like the big Christmas present she turned out to be, and discovered a long, lean vessel 25 feet overall, but with only a 6 1/2-foot beam. Even at first glance — and in spite of peeling paint and varnish, open planking seams, and damage from an encounter with a piling — there was no mistaking the work of one of the world's great geniuses of sailing yacht design. She was all about the easy passage of water around a hull. She had been smooth-planked in African mahogany. These planks spanned the full length of the boat with no need for butt blocks and their seams. The planks were originally fitted tightly

ture is present. Light was visible through the open plank seams, but this provided some natural ventilation, which was good news.

More thumping and probing on the inside of the hull — paying special attention to the area in the bilge next to the oak plank keel batten — turned up nothing but healthy wood. The bad news within the hull was a good number of broken oak frames. The apparent lack of rot was a little surprising, as the owner stated that the boat always had at least a foot of water in the bilge when at her mooring. It was easy to see how all that water had gotten there. The 3/8-inch, seven-ply mahogany plywood decks had no covering of any sort — neither fiberglass nor canvas. As the streaks staining the hull sides showed, rain was finding its way in at the deck and hull joint. Also, the hull's open planking seams must have leaked in swells and boat wakes. By far though, the largest amount of water had probably entered from the cockpit, which was not self-draining. One might rightly ask, "Why didn't she just sink?" This question would ultimately lead to the most difficult single decision concerning the boat's restoration.

For a period of time starting in the mid 1970s, the boat was owned by a skipper who traveled from Chicago to Charlevoix, Michigan to use her. His visits took place only once a summer for three consecutive weeks. The boat spent the rest of the time hauled out on shore, drying out in the wind. The owner would call the boatyard ahead of time so they could have her in the water upon his arrival. Of course she would leak to the point of sinking through her open seams. Since the owner wanted to sail and not pump, he decided to apply about eight layers of fiberglass cloth (using an early epoxy resin) over the hull and keel starting just above the waterline. The topsides were just painted. This remedy provided a relatively dry boat for the owner when launched, but didn't keep rain water, which leaked through the decks and cockpit, from accumulating in the bilge. Of course, water came in through the still open planking seams above the waterline any time the boat heeled over. As I was soon to learn, this fiberglass covering both helped and hurt the boat.

After looking the boat over, my wife and I looked at each other. Then we looked back at the boat. My mind and heart were at war with each other. I should say that I was no stranger to boats and boatbuilding. I well understood the endless hours a restoration can consume, and the countless decisions that have to be made. What would my vision for the boat be? How far and in what direction would I take a restoration? Would I want to use the boat when done or perhaps try to sell it? You might think I'd know better than to undertake yet another project like this one. In the end, however, I was unable to resist such a challenge. My decision boiled down to this: "Is this boat worth the effort involved?" Whether it was for the challenge or for the pleasure of saving something beautiful from the chain saw, or just the simple joy of working with such gorgeous mahogany, I bought her on the spot.

On a perfect Easter Sunday morning in 2000, we dragged *Sante* home on the trailer she'd lived on for so many years. The trailer was an immense double-axle, welded steel affair weighing twice the weight of the boat. My 10-year-old, four-cylinder Toyota pickup seemed just adequate for the task.

As a 25-foot boat wouldn't fit in the garage, I decided to position the trailer off to the side of our gravel driveway. She wound up with the stern about six feet away from the house. The first thing I did was to rig up a light cable. It was anchored on one end to a hook screwed into the fascia of the house. The other end connected to a vertical pipe on the front end of the trailer which extended above the bow and was designed to support the mast. Next I draped a large plastic tarp over a ridgepole that ran from bow to stern. While working on the boat, I could spread the sides of the tarp to make a big tent. At night, the

The Junior Holiday's fine lines, if not her narrow beam, are evident in this profile view of the boat as she appeared before restoration began.

a boat that could be patched together and used for a few years? My personality greatly influenced the answers to these questions. I know myself well enough to know that I just can't patch things together. On the other side of the coin, I also knew that I didn't want to get bogged down in a five-year, x-ray-every-screw-and-bolt, museum quality restoration.

There was no doubt that the boat was a very important example of a 1950s performance cruiser designed by a master, but she wasn't a museum piece. She was intended to be built numerous times, most likely from patterns, at a reasonable cost, and to look great and sail even better.

It would be wonderful to say that after all this ruminating I came up with a rock-solid plan for the boat and that I adhered to it. But this didn't happen. I did come to some conclusions though:

1) The boat was no basket case. There was a good sound structure to work with.
2) With modern construction methods, I could make her stronger than when originally built, and hopefully leak-free.
3) I knew that I wanted to make every effort to preserve her 1956 style to honor her original design.
4) I had a block of time available and could stay right at her until finished, which fits my work ethic.
5) Since I would learn much more about the boat as time went on, I knew the plan would have to adapt, but within the stated objectives.

By the time I began this project, I had built and

tarp could be tied back down to the trailer. On good weather days, I could dispense with the cover altogether. The benefits of my outside work space included its close access to the garage, which I used as a shop, and unlimited fresh air for all those dusty and smelly operations. The major negative point to this arrangement, at least from Marie's perspective, turned out to be the noise of power tools so close to the house and her studio window. I'm not so sure I would have been as tolerant as she turned out to be.

A good first step for me, and an exciting one, was to get up inside and give her a good cleaning out. All sorts of items collect in the bilge of a boat over the years, so instead of using a shop-vac to suck up everything, I went about slowly looking for treasures. I was a bit disappointed to find only the odd assortment of nuts and washers, a couple of rusty screwdrivers, cotter pins, bobby pins, and small and medium sized pieces of wood, which I saved. After vacuuming up the remaining dirt, leaves, and indefinables, I just sat back against the side of the hull and had a good long look and think.

Now that I really knew what I was dealing with, I asked myself what was my vision for the boat? What kind of restoration to undertake? Was she a classic that deserved a complete rebuild or

restored a number of boats. Based on that experience, I knew that the best chance of a successful restoration depended on a realistic plan. This seems an obvious point, but I think many of us have seen projects of all types started with no plan whatsoever. It's sometimes tempting to proceed with an attitude that says, "I'll just tear into her and see what happens." This approach, however, almost never leads to success; it may end with a boat that never sees the water again. On the other hand, there have been many inexperienced men and women, and even teenagers, who through a kind of orderly, steadfast persistence have achieved incredible results, with a level of workmanship that would be the envy of any professional boat builder.

To get a better handle on things, I spent the next few days getting to know the boat in an effort to find as many of her problems and her good features as I could. I hoped the boat could tell me what she needed. The list of first priority items included:

1) Broken frames. What to do about the great number of these? Something like 80 percent of the frames were broken, many in more than one place.
2) Open planking seams. Some seams gaped as much as 1/4-inch. The glue used to bond the planks together had failed due to expansion and contraction of the planks themselves. (The steam-bent frames, attached to the planks with screws, doubtless had been too small in section and couldn't resist this force, so they fractured.)
3) The fiberglass below the waterline. Leave it or take it off?
4) The engine. This was a 1956 one-cylinder, 7-hp Palmer BH. Should I repair it or remove it permanently?
5) The cockpit. The cockpit was not self-draining. Several attempts had been made by others to keep water from leaking into the bilge of the boat by adding an additional floor over the original one. Removing the whole mess and replacing it with a proper self-draining cockpit, complete with seats and lockers, was probably the best option.
6) The decks. These were 3/8-inch mahogany marine plywood and had been varnished originally. Should I glass them?
7) The hull above the waterline. Should I strip off all the paint and finish all that beautiful mahogany bright?

The list went on including many more items of descending importance. Knowing what I had to deal with, I made a few tentative decisions.

My plan was to first get the engine out of the boat. Lacking a suitable tree limb to hoist from, I substituted two ladders lashed together at the top and spread out on the bottom spanning the

A pair of wooden step ladders formed a makeshift but functional A-frame with which the engine could be hoisted.

boat. After adding a few lines to steady this makeshift A-frame, I hooked up a tackle. I disconnected wiring, shaft, exhaust, mounting bolts, and fuel lines. I hauled the engine clear of the boat. It was at this point that I decided not to reinstall it. The engine impressed me as being much too heavy for this fine-lined boat. What's more, the space it took up could be used to build a proper cockpit. The previous owner had not even used the engine, choosing to hang an outboard motor from the stern. Next, I used a scraper and putty knife to remove as much of the grease and grunge from the engine compartment as possible. I then used rags soaked in lacquer thinner to mop up the rest. The welded steel engine mount came out next along with the copper exhaust lines, control cables, wiring, rusted fuel tank, stuffing box, shaft, and propeller.

Over the next few days, I removed everything possible from the boat: all deck and sailing hardware, interior bulkheads and partitions, bunk dividers, rub and toe rails, hatches, rudder, handrails, and all through-hulls. I made notes for each item as it was removed, noting location and reference measurements from a given point. If I had it to do over again, I would take photographs — lots of them. They would have helped me greatly and, in the event that my life situation changed, these photos would have enabled someone else to take over where I left off. Hardware items had their fasteners taped or wired to them, and were packed away in boxes for later cleaning and reinstallation. At this time, however, I removed nothing that would have compromised the structural integrity of the boat. For example, no frames, main bulkheads, or decks were disturbed.

It was now time to closely examine the boat to see if she had held her shape. In the past I had encountered boats with long, drooping overhangs at bow and stern. Many times the eye can spot these abnormal lines or curves first, and then measurements can be made from a level plane to confirm the amount of distortion. Gentle, sustained pressure can often make things right again. I have used 2 x 4s propped under the rub rails, stem, or stern to create this kind of pressure; putting a wedge under them and tapping it every day to exert more force. Gentle and slow is the answer here, just as it probably took a long time for these deformities in the hull to occur. If the hull won't take its proper shape using the above method, then one might have to remove a few planks to release the pressure. I counted myself fortunate that *Sante* had kept her shape over the years and was well supported by the trailer.

Next, I removed the entire cockpit, thereby exposing the true result of attempts by many "remuddlers" to make the boat watertight. What I discovered was a real mess of interior plywood and common lumber all held together with fiberglass, resin, house caulk, and almost every kind of nail or screw imaginable. This was one time when I was forced to violate the prime directive of restoration work, which states: "Save every piece... intact if possible." Usually pieces of a boat, even if they are rotten and will not go back into the boat, hold a wealth of information locked up in their surfaces. They can be used as patterns. The time spent carefully removing them will be repaid many times over when fitting new parts. This boat's cockpit, however, was a lost cause. Out it went!

Eventually, my initial disassembly process came to an end. I realized that I was getting to know the boat and to appreciate how well she had been built. I was also very surprised — and pleased — to find no rot in the boat's basic hull structure.

In order to decide what to do about the broken frames, I inventoried the fractures by sticking a piece of masking tape to each one. The end result revealed a pattern of stress concentrated at or above the waterline. There were none below where the hull had been glassed, limiting plank movement. Above the waterline the planks had alternately swelled, shrunk, and cracked the frames straight across. All these frames would have to be replaced. I made a plan to laminate new frames directly into the boat using six to eight laminations of 1/8" x 1 1/4" ash with epoxy as an adhesive. Before this could be done, however, I needed to deal with the open plank seams or they would be locked in. I used various thin blades to remove the debris and paint from them, taking care not to damage the faces of the planks. Of course one thing leads to another, and as I had decided to make an attempt to finish the topsides bright (varnished), more than a dozen coats of white paint would have to come off.

Under no circumstances is stripping paint an enjoyable experience. I tried everything from chemical strippers, scrapers, hot air guns, and various sanders. I don't think an easy way exists. What seemed to work for me was a very carefully controlled four-inch grinder with 50-grit paper to remove the bulk of the paint, but never down to bare wood. A random orbit sander was used next, working up through the grits to expose the gorgeous African mahogany. A good quality dust mask was a necessity. This process took approximately 50 hours.

Mahogany bungs covered the bronze screws holding the planking to the frames. These bungs had to come out in order to remove the fasteners. I split the bungs out with a very small chisel using much care to keep from splitting or chipping the plank face. Alternatively, one can drill an 1/8-inch hole in the center of the bung down to the screw and then drive a screw in that hole. This should back the bung right out, but sometimes it takes the edges of the planking along with it.

I had been wondering if some of the wider spaces where the glue had failed between planks would close up if I could just put some pressure on the hull. If the boat had been in a building, I might have used props from the rafters to exert downward force against the sheer plank at the deck edge. Instead, the trailer frame would serve as a place to anchor one end of a strap with the other end attached to the deck and deck beams with screws. To my surprise, when the strain was taken up using the ratcheting mechanism of the straps, most of the seams closed substantially.

Now was the time to start replacing frames. I replaced them one at a time to preserve the hull shape. The drill was as follows:

1) Remove the screws holding the planking to the frame in question. They could not be removed below the waterline because of the fiberglass covering.
2) Split the frames out of the boat with a chisel and mallet.
3) Grind the protruding screws located below the waterline flush with the hull. The remaining part of the screw would stay in the plank trapped between the fiberglass covering on the outside and the new frame on the inside.
4) Clean the area under the rib with a scraper and grinder so that it would later accept epoxy.
5) Cut and dry fit the ash laminations.
6) Mix epoxy and filler to a mayonnaise consistency.
7) Butter up the laminations one at a time placing them against the hull.
8) Brace them to the hull from convenient places on the opposite side of the boat using 2" x 2" lumber. Depending on the curvature of the hull, a few or many braces were needed.
9) Make certain that the laminations were in alignment and snugged down tight to the hull and each other.
10) Drive screws from the planking side into the new frame, using the existing holes. In most cases I could use the original bronze screws. Below the waterline, I bored holes for screws through the fiberglass and planking.
11) Clean up the excess epoxy.
12) Move on to the same frame on the opposite side of the boat.

In practice, this proved to be messy, slippery work. An adequate supply of rags and solvent was a necessity to mop up spills. Despite taking every precaution, it is surprisingly easy to walk or kneel in spilled liquids and wind up tracking it all over the boat. Safety is also important. Although most epoxy has little odor it is still toxic stuff. A quality respirator and protection for skin and eyes are mandatory. The same is true for any sanding operations. I can't emphasize this enough. The 3M™ Company manufactures quality safety equipment. As for gloves, don't rely on thin latex ones for any extended work as they tear easily. I have had great luck with thick Playtex™ dishwashing gloves. They are a bit clumsy, but cured epoxy can be peeled right off them, allowing them to be used over and over again.

After the epoxy had cured, I used a belt sander, rasp, and 80-grit sandpaper to clean up the frames and round over the sharp edges. After that, I applied four coats of unthickened epoxy. One after another the old frames came out and the new went in until finally there were no more to replace. It was a relief to be done with this process as the headroom in the boat was only 50 inches and I, at six feet three inches, had acquired quite a few knocks on my head and a chronic sore back.

I now cut new bungs using scrap mahogany from the cockpit, which matched the planking material. These were dipped in varnish and tapped into the screw counter bores, taking care to align them with the grain in the planking. A sharp chisel and sandpaper were used to cut them down flush with the hull. Below the waterline, the screw holes in the fiberglass were filled with thickened epoxy. By now you will have guessed that I had decided to leave the fiberglass covering on. I had wrestled with this decision for some time and had arrived at a conclusion based on the following:

1) The covering was bonded tenaciously to the planking.

2) The resin used with the fiberglass cloth was epoxy, which is much stronger than polyester and is far superior in keeping moisture out of wood.

3) The hull could be leak-free if I glassed the decks and built a self-draining cockpit.

4) The substantial covering added considerable stiffness to the hull and probably was part of the reason the boat had so little distortion.

I realized that there were all sorts of opinions about fiberglass on wood boats, but in the end I knew that the boat had had its covering for at least 20 years. It still stuck like crazy despite the boat being full of water all the time. There was absolutely no rot evident in the hull. This is not a blanket approval of glass on wood, but in this case, there was no arguing that it had been a success.

Now that the planking was stabilized on new frames, I thickened some epoxy with fine mahogany sanding dust obtained from the orbital sander, and using a putty knife filled in the now much smaller planking seam openings. This took several attempts to make sure all seams were completely filled. Perhaps the widest of these openings was 1/8-inch. After a comprehensive sanding of the topsides with an orbital sander using 80-, 150-, and finally 220-grit paper, I made a close inspection of the hull to be sure no paint remained. Next, six successive coats of epoxy were applied with a plastic squeegee originally intended for applying vinyl letters. After curing, each coat was wet sanded with 150-grit paper and the hull washed down with fresh water. Later, I would apply many coats of varnish because epoxy has no ultraviolet protection.

A design for a new self-draining cockpit, complete with seats and storage lockers, had been percolating in my brain almost since the work began. I intended to build the cockpit of 1/2-inch marine plywood with an epoxy, six-ounce fiberglass cloth overlay. The steps in the construction were as follows:

1) Build a mockup using wood strips to delineate the floor, seat levels, and bridge deck. This allowed me to visualize the cockpit better and make a few changes, such as raising the sole (floor) to an appropriate height above the waterline for drainage.
2) Cut out the various parts with circular and scroll saws.
3) Dry fit these parts together using drywall screws as temporary fasteners.
4) Lay the parts out flat, smoothing out fiberglass cloth over them, and applying the first coat of epoxy.
5) Flow a second coat of epoxy on the panels after the first coat had tacked, filling the weave in one operation. When done on a horizontal plane, this can result in a glass-like surface that requires minimal sanding. There are no runs to deal with and no building up of coats.
6) Reassemble the parts after they were glassed and sanded on their outside surfaces. I thickened the epoxy fillets at joints with several layers of six-ounce fiberglass tape. (The fillets are just small radiuses of thickened epoxy that act like welds.)

I made a very interesting discovery during the work on the cockpit. While removing one of the original solid mahogany seats, from an inaccessible place on the underside, I found the boat's name — *Sante* — painted several times in the same blue and in the same style as on the transom. I suspect that the sign painter was practicing before painting the name for real on the stern. Also, the name had been painted on the bare mahogany of the transom and then varnished over. This is a little unusual; it's usually done the other way around. This all leads me to believe that the boat has carried the same name for its whole life, which is most unusual.

The process of working with epoxy and fiberglass cloth is not complicated, but it falls under the category of "read and heed" regarding manufacturer's instructions. I have found that instruction manuals from brands such as West System™ or System Three™ are most helpful. There are other good brands of epoxy out there, but these two companies have been around for a long time, have excellent tech support, and have done extensive product testing.

Even if you have little or no experience with these materials, you can rely upon the instructions to help you become proficient. A few points of emphasis are in order:

1) Minimum safety equipment includes a respirator and substantial gloves. Wear them!
2) Every minute spent cleaning up excess epoxy before it cures will save you one half hour sanding and scraping cured epoxy.
3) Adhesive tape and plastic sheeting help keep epoxy from getting where you don't want it. For instance, when filleting plywood panels together, use tape to delineate the fillet.
4) If using fiberglass cloth with epoxy, make certain that they are compatible with each other. Any reputable supplier will be able to answer this question for you.

I set about tackling the decks next. The toe rail — a 3/4-inch-square mahogany piece of trim running the full length of the deck edge — and the rub rail — 1" x 2" mahogany, also full length and located at the upper limit of the hull — had been removed earlier. These both had been screwed and bunged to the boat. There were about 10 places on the deck where delamination of the 3/8-inch marine plywood was evident, including areas around the chain plates, hatches, and deck edges. These areas were carefully cut back to solid plies and given tapering sides with a block plane and sharp chisel. Pieces were then cut from similar plywood to match the openings. There are many ways to obtain good fits. Patterns made using a relatively stiff but translucent paper worked for me. Cut the pieces a little big all around and sand them to fit with a belt sander. Epoxy thickened with sanding dust was used to glue them in place. I remembered to clean up the epoxy that had oozed out under the deck.

After the epoxy had cured, I sanded down the decks to bare wood using belt and orbital sanders. Scrapers were employed where sanders could not reach. After the decks were fair, smooth, and cleaned, six-ounce fiberglass cloth was laid out over them, wrapping the edges over the gunwale so the rub rail would cover the edge when reinstalled. I butted the cloth against the solid mahogany cabin sides. Epoxy resin was applied using the float coat method previously described. After 48 hours or so, I gave the surface a good sanding, filled any hollows or imperfections with thickened epoxy, and sanded them flush. The boat's three hatches — companionway, stern, and foredeck — were given similar treatment by sanding to bare wood, repairing damage and loose joints with epoxy, and then glassing them.

Though I had been dreading it, I couldn't avoid the area below the waterline any longer. All traces of bottom paint had to come off in order to grind and fair the fiberglass-epoxy covering. I lay on my back and went at it, using scrapers, grinder, sanders, and blistering language. Bottom paint is very toxic to the environment and to you, so I recommend spreading plastic sheeting beneath the boat to collect as much of the dust and particles as possible. You can then dispose of this in a responsible way. Your city or township might have a toxic waste collection point. If not, call your local waste collector for advice. A respirator and protection for skin and eyes are again absolutely mandatory. Use a shop vac to blow yourself off before entering any living space.

As an alternative to mechanical removal of bottom paint, there are paint strippers specifically intended for bottom paints. Although expensive, these do a good job at containment. A valid argument can be made, however, that this increases the amount of hazardous material to be dealt with. It was a happy day when all this paint was off the boat.

A good deal of work was necessary to fair out the existing glass covering of the bottom. Again, thickened epoxy was used for this. I applied it with a wide trowel and after curing, I sanded it with a belt sander, grinder, and finally a "long board". A "long board' is nothing but a piece of 1/4-inch plywood about 6"x 30" with sandpaper glued or stapled to it. Handles on each end let you move it back and forth on a surface. It will bend to the surface thereby wearing down unseen high spots. There is a love-hate relationship between boat builders and this tool. They love it because it does such a great job, but hate it for the amount of physical effort needed to use it. Go ahead, join the fun, and make your own board with the degree of flexibility and shape your boat requires. I repeated this process of applying epoxy and then sanding quite a number of times until the hull was finally smooth and fair.

The 30-inch by 15-inch spade rudder had been made from one piece of solid mahogany lumber. With the passage of time it had cupped in a horizontal direction. I built up the hollow side with laminations of the same wood and epoxy. I used a plane on the proud side to restore symmetry. The one-inch bronze rudder shaft was ground down to bare metal. Then the whole works was wrapped in three layers of fiberglass cloth and epoxy, flow-coating each side. After sanding and fairing with a little thickened epoxy, then sanding again, I reinstalled the rudder on the boat.

Over the next weeks, multiple coats of spar varnish were applied to topsides, cabin sides, rub and toe rails, hand rails, mast and boom, wood cleats, and most of the previously removed wooden items. Most of these pieces could be varnished in the garage, but the boat had to be dealt with where it was. The procedure for the hull was as follows:

1) Wet sand with 220-grit paper.
2) Wash with water then dry the topsides.
3) Apply a thin coat of varnish with a 3-inch foam brush after cleaning surfaces with a tack rag. (I have always preferred Z-Spar Captain's Varnish™).
4) Repeat the process the next day, or when the weather allows. I avoided windy days or days that threatened rain. Remember though, the perfect climatic conditions called for on the varnish label do not exist, or at least not in my area. I built up ten coats using this method. Each morning I would inspect the previous day's coat expecting to see varnish that looked like flypaper, but would find a near perfect surface. The relatively thin amount applied by foam brush and all the fresh air surrounding the boat allowed the varnish to dry very quickly, getting the jump on the bugs.

The decks were primed and painted with my favorite Benjamin Moore alkyd enamel. I chose a very light buff color that would be easy on the eyes in the sun. I mixed in a product called Skid-Tex™, available at most paint stores, for areas that required a non-skid surface. These areas were masked off from surfaces where just paint was applied.

It was now time to strike the waterline, which required that the boat be leveled fore, aft, and athwartships. I used a level clamped to a straight board to bridge the distance across the boat. I placed this board on similar points on the deck edge of each side of the hull for reference points. Fortunately the boat was supported on the trailer with screw-type jacks, which could be adjusted until she was level across her beam. The wheeled jack stand on the trailer tongue was cranked up or down as necessary to level the boat longitudinal-

ly. Much of this work had been done earlier to allow the cockpit to be built square and plumb with the boat. I used an electronic water level to set the upper and lower limits of the white boot top. This inexpensive tool is available at most hardware stores and makes short work of striking waterlines. A home builder's laser level could also be used. Three coats of paint were applied to the boot, sanding between coats with 220-grit paper.

Next I reassembled the cabin interior, put floorboards back in, reinstalled deck and sailing hardware, screwed down toe and rub rails, bolted on hand rails, etc. Dolphinite marine bedding compound was used between these items and the surfaces they were fastened to in an effort to prevent leaks and rot. I avoided using any silicone product for this purpose because it bleeds away from the fitting, lifting the paint from around it. Also, do not use a polyurethane product such as 3M 5200 for bedding topside components or hardware. It's great below the waterline, but it's not good for any item that may have to be removed in the future as it bonds tenaciously to most surfaces.

On rainy days, or when waiting for epoxy, paint, or varnish to dry, I would devote time to other components. These included:

1) *Mast and boom.* The sitka spruce mast and boom were original to the boat and were in exceptional shape. They needed only to have their hardware items removed, and to be sanded down prior to varnishing.
2) *The cockpit drains.* I installed Marelon™ through- hull fittings and sea cocks, connecting them up with a good grade of hose and double stainless steel hose clamps.
3) *A 12-volt electrical system.* This was kept as simple as possible and included a small distribution panel, battery box, rewiring of the original side and stern lights, one small cabin light, and the installation of a 12" x 16" solar panel to recharge the battery.

4) *Cushions.* This included making paper patterns for the foam berth cushions and sewing new covers.

5) *Outboard motor bracket.* I built a laminated wood outboard motor bracket, though it would never be used.

6) *Sink.* I installed the original galvanized-steel 10-gallon fresh water tank, the small stainless steel sink with plumbing, and the Whale™ foot pump.

7) *Bilge.* This entailed fitting a high capacity hand bilge pump in one of the cockpit lockers. As the bilge of this boat was relatively flat, there needed to be a lot of water in the boat before the bilge pump would work. Consequently, I decided to chisel out a 6" x 8" x 8" sump directly down into the deadwood of the keel. This was given numerous coats of epoxy and fiberglass cloth. After it cured, I put the intake hose of the pump into it. Any water coming into the boat accumulated in this sump first. In practice, the helmsperson could open the cockpit locker and take a few strokes on the pump handle to find out if the boat was dry. This turned out to be a great consolation on dark, stormy nights.

8) *Tiller.* The tiller, laminated of mahogany and ash, had to be reglued and varnished.

9) *Trailer.* I removed about 1,000 pounds of unnecessary steel from the trailer. The previous owner launched the boat directly from the trailer; there was an elaborate system of steel keel guides as well a 30-foot steel A-frame

with counterweights to raise the mast. All this was cut away with a reciprocating saw. The trailer also needed to be rewired.

10) *Rigging.* The wire head stay, back stay, and shrouds had been poorly done in 1/8-inch wire. I made replacement rigging using 5/32-inch, 1 x 19 stainless steel wire with hydraulically swaged fittings.

Gradually, the list of items to be completed shrank. Anyone who has owned a boat knows that this list never reaches zero. There are always little spots to be touched up or small changes to be made. For me, a good part of the enjoyment of owning a wooden boat is knowing that you are never really finished. Working on the boat and experimenting gives great satisfaction.

When I took the tarps off *Sante* in the spring of 2001, after not being able to see the whole boat for the previous six months, I could do nothing but stare silently at Mr. van de Stadt's creation. I'd been so close to the work for so long that the overall result came as a surprise. In hindsight, I view the project as something of a privilege. How often does one get to work on a boat so well designed and built?

A "small" 25-footer, the Junior Holiday possessed a fin keel configuration, spade rudder, and narrow beam that were highlights of van de Stadt post-war design.

Almost one year to the day of her purchase, *Sante* was launched at a marina on Lake Michigan. She was watertight from the start, and the first rain proved the cockpit drained properly and the decks and chain plates no longer leaked. After stepping the mast for the first time, my immediate impression was that the boat was under canvassed. This equates to a lack of horsepower in a powerboat. I couldn't have been more wrong.

The first sail proved that Mr. van de Stadt had nailed this design dead on. The forces on a hull and rig of a sailing boat make themselves evident by the pressure needed to be applied to the rudder to steer a straight course. Lots of pressure in one direction or another usually means a hull and rig that are out of balance with each other. With this boat, there were perhaps one or two pounds of pull on the tiller whether sailing in five knots of wind or 30! This balance is something that boat designers strive for their whole careers. Many come close but only a few succeed completely, and then maybe with only one design. In addition, the boat was quite fast and would sail very close to the wind. The combination of these wonderful characteristics, and the fact that she lay on a mooring, made the outboard motor unnecessary. After using the brand new four-hp Johnson only once, I took it ashore permanently.

Sante was sailed a lot that first summer, primarily on Lake Michigan. And she was sailed hard. Several times I was caught out in 35-knot wind and the Lake's famous 10-foot square waves. Although I was a bit apprehensive at first, I need not have been for the boat eased herself through it all with a minimum of fuss, no pounding, and always under perfect control. I guess all boat owners brag about their vessel's ability, but *Sante* amazed me. *Sante* was by far the most well-behaved boat I have ever had the privilege of sailing.

When hauled out at the end of a leak-free season, I inspected *Sante*

Author Kaphaem reports that the Junior Holiday possessed perfect balance, rarely needing more than a light touch on the tiller no matter what the wind velocity.

With her bright-finished hull, this beautiful sailboat emerged as a tribute to Steve Kaphaem's vision and skill.

carefully for cracks in plank seams or any other signs of stress. There were none. At the time of this writing, she continues to be sailed on the Great Lakes and is lovingly cared for by her present owner.

BOAT SPECS:

Designer	E. G. van de Stadt
Design	#41 Junior Holiday (Victoria, in Europe)
Year Built	1956
Length OA x LWL x beam x draft	24'8" x 17' 8 1/2" x 6'6" x 4'
Construction	Glued-seam mahogany planks over oak frames
Displacement	2,650 lbs.
Rig	Marconi 7/8ths rig, 200 square feet
Cost	$2,000 purchase plus $2,500 spent on restoration

TOOL LIST

I would consider these the basics:

- Assorted-size screwdrivers
- Chisels
- Hammer
- Various scrapers
- Block plane
- Bevel gauge
- Square
- Level
- 7 1/4" circular saw
- Random orbit sander
- 4-inch angle grinder
- Belt sander
- 3/8-inch electric drill and bits
- Lots of clamps of different sizes
- A set of small wrenches.

A table saw or band saw would be put to good use but wouldn't be absolutely necessary. My personal feeling is that it doesn't make economic sense for most of us to go out and collect a whole bunch of tools in the hope we might use them, but rather buy the right tool when the need arises. If you don't expect to use a particular tool again in the future, and if it's rather expensive, perhaps renting makes more sense.

About the Author: Born in 1946, Steve Kaphaem has been fascinated by all kinds of boats and ships since age five or six. He has designed, built, and worked on boats all his life and estimates that he has accumulated 125,000 sailing miles. Besides boatbuilding, Steve is a self-employed carpenter. He has also worked as a farmhand and theater set builder. He lives with his Canadian-born wife Marie Lamothe, a watercolor artist, and their 22-pound cat, Bubba, in northern Michigan.

7

An Old Town Runabout

BY KEN DEADY

Best known for the wood and canvas canoes it began building at the start of the 20th century, the Old Town Canoe Company also built kayaks and some very highly regarded all-wood runabouts. Introduced in 1931, the 16-foot Ocean Boat had a 60-inch beam, nine inches greater than the otherwise similar Sea Model. That added width, said the company, "makes the boat come out of the water quicker and plane better with large motors." Doubtless, this Ocean Boat was about as able a 16-footer as one was likely to find, then or now. Built of cedar over oak and ash ribs, brass-screw fastened, and with a varnished interior, these shapely Old Towns were also beautiful. Production continued through 1956. Lest we forget that a boat like this can become a member of the family, this chapter will serve as a strong reminder.

One of my earliest and fondest childhood memories is of a beautiful spring Sunday in 1967. That was the day when I first spotted the boat that would become a member of our family. "Look at that!" I said as we drove past a 16-foot runabout parked by the side of the road in Framingham, Massachusetts. A For Sale sign was prominently displayed. To reassure my father, who'd been looking at boats for some time but wouldn't consider a fiberglass model, I added, "I don't think that's a fiberglass boat."

Dad responded by immediately turning around. The boat was uncovered and we were immediately impressed by the varnished interior and the white topsides. The owner told us that this was a 1933 Old Town Ocean Boat and that his $300 asking price included the old, but serviceable, 25-hp Johnson outboard motor and a custom trailer. Although we might not have appreciated it at the time, we were actually looking at a completely equipped antique runabout that, thanks to having been boathouse-stored for 30 years on an estate in Wellesley, Massachusetts, was completely intact. In fact, the boat had always been well maintained with paint and varnish as prescribed in the owner's information supplied by Old Town.

The runabout was constructed from cedar strips and steam bent oak ribs in a style derived from Old Town's legendary canoes. The hull's

"Old Town" ALL-WOOD OCEANBOAT

"...capable of carrying the largest motors under extremely unfavorable weather conditions," is how Old Town described its 16' Ocean Boat. The company noted the "floor frame and transom are built extra heavy" and their claims were supported by customers.

complex shape — a plumb bow tapering gracefully to the stern with its elegant tumblehome — is even more distinctive today than it was in the '30s. It's a hull with many subtleties that, we soon learned, contributed to a smooth ride and good performance. The boat had a mahogany foredeck, gunwales, and splash rail running from bow to stern on the waterline. The fastenings were copper rivets and bronze screws. Hardware included a bronze Samson post on the foredeck, two bronze lifting rings on the stern quarters, and a pair of pop-up oar locks.

The interior was fitted with two forward-facing folding seats and two rear-facing seats where, originally, the operator could sit and steer with a hand on the motor's tiller. The seats were made of inch-thick pine and still included the kapok cushions. Records we received with the boat indicated that in 1936 running lights, a decorative bronze windshield, chocks, as well as a steering wheel and bronze pulley system were added to bring the outfit to the configuration it had when we purchased it.

The first season of boating with the old green Johnson Seahorse was quite memorable. At a tender young age, I learned the colorful vocabulary common to engine rooms around the world as my father, a retired US Navy engineer officer, would issue the complex commands, also colorful, necessary for a seven year old to keep the fuel mix adjusted properly while speeding up or slowing down. Failure do so resulted in fouled plugs,

broken sheer pins, and spectacular invocations of ill will to all things mechanical. I got pretty good at this routine and we had a lot of great cruises despite the breakdowns.

Our third season began with a new Mercury Twin 35-hp motor and a new name for the boat. We christened the boat the *DD-5*, a nod to the five members of the Deady family and my father's former service as an engineering officer aboard destroyers. Aboard the *DD-5*, we cruised lakes in Massachusetts, New Hampshire, and Maine, exploring just about any body of water with a launching ramp. The boat was also regularly used for water skiing and cruising up and down the Charles River into Boston Harbor and up the Mystic River as a regular tour. It was in attendance at Boston's Tall Ships festivals, Boston Pops concerts, and Boston's July fourth celebrations, with the 1976 season being among the wildest experiences we have ever had.

After the 1977 season, the boat became neglected when the crew left home to go to college. At this time my parents moved from Massachusetts to New Hampshire. The boat moved with them but, in the absence of a big enough garage, was now stored outside. Then my father suffered a heart attack and the boat began to suffer from neglect. When I inspected our Old Town in 1980, I decided to do a cosmetic refurbishing. With a few gallons of 5f5, arguably the best chemical stripper ever, 50 years of marine paint blistered away leaving the cleanest wood I have ever seen. This process also revealed the original colors (white sides, forest green bottom, and clear varnish interior), intact Old Town decal logos on both stern quarters, and even the original name, *Mary A*. We also discovered beautifully painted registration numbers on the bow.

Removal of the bronze hardware revealed maker and casting marks from Wilcox Crittenden and Co. and Elco. Serial numbers on the running lights and some research in old parts catalogs also verified the age of the accessory parts. With the help of a few friends, we flipped over the boat, filled cracks with "goo", and repainted the hull. An electric winch was now installed on the trailer to ease launch and retrieval so that Captain Jack, my father, could once again use the boat. We repowered the boat twice during the next few years.

All was well until 1992. Then, thieves cut the 1990 25-hp Mercury from the transom, damaging the boat and breaking my father's heart. With cables and wire hanging over the transom, the boat was towed to a barn in New Hampshire for storage. There it remained until 1997 when, in a phone conversation, my father mentioned that he'd had the boat appraised and was finally going to sell it. By then, I was living in Florida and it was not until a couple of days later that I received a copy of the appraisal and some pictures. Our old Old Town had clearly fallen on hard times. Still, the boat seemed like a member of the family and it was hard to think of it actually going somewhere else.

It had been 16 years since my modest refinishing project. I had no idea, when that work was done, that my father would still be around after a few more heart attacks and surgeries — but he was. Now, as a tribute to them both — dad had been born in 1933 and was the same vintage as the boat — I decided to do a full restoration of the *DD-5*. This time, I knew I would have my work cut out for me and would need to give extra attention to problems that had previously been skipped or merely painted over. With the idea of

"going cruising with The Old Man again," I began to make plans to make that dream come true for both of us.

STARTING OUT

The first challenge was to get a fragile boat and decrepit trailer from Bedford, New Hampshire, to St. Petersburg, Florida. I began by calling some of the major moving companies for quotes and getting some references of those specializing in boat hauling and delivery. After many outrageous quotes and estimated dates of arrival of "some time", I called Dallas & Mavis Specialized Carrier in Jacksonville. They were looking to balance a load from Manchester, New Hampshire to Florida. We discussed the shape and size of the boat and trailer and the truckers agreed that the Old Town could be nestled in the middle of their load of special hurricane resistant poles for a nice safe trip. The estimate for pick up and delivery was three weeks and, with this motivation, my father arranged to have the boat semi-stripped and packaged for shipping.

The boat was then towed to a local boat yard in Hooksett, New Hampshire. There, a fork lift placed the boat and trailer onto the flat-bed trailer. Three days later, the *DD-5* was delivered to the Maximo High and Dry Boat Yard about one mile from my home. The driver, Marty Lash, was great. I could not have had the delivery in better hands. The folks at Maximo High and Dry were more than happy to unload the boat for me to tow home. The boat hauling cost $1,000 plus a $500 tip for the driver — money well spent.

Before the boat arrived, I cleaned out the garage and arranged my tools and work space so that I could begin work immediately. With the boat safely at her new home, the first step was to unpack and organize all of the parts and hardware. Every screw and piece of hardware was removed, labeled, and stored in zip-lock bags of the appropriate size. In fact, each piece would eventually become a small individual tabletop restoration project of its own. Taking care in this very first step of the project paid off because nothing was lost. And, when one's memory fails, the label tells you (or someone else) exactly what you're dealing with and where on the boat it was located.

After the removal of the running hardware, careful disassembly of the structural accessories was the next step. This process included taking out the seats and their supports, cross braces, floorboards, and any hardware attached to them. Because all of the wooden pieces would require refinishing, I wanted to be sure they were neatly and safely stored, so I constructed a dual-purpose storage and drying rack resembling a giant saw horse. I built this rack out of 2" x 4" x 8' lumber and outfitted it with eye screws at four-inch intervals. Each piece of floorboard, seat, and support was also fitted with an eye screw at the point of best balance and hung on long hooks fashioned from trimmed and bent coat hangers. This method of storing and drying the parts proved

This storage and drying rack was built early in the project and proved to be exceptionally useful in producing professional results during the finishing of individual parts.

very efficient and looked quite professional to visitors.

It's worth noting that, as I removed all these parts, I discovered several that would need replacement. These included the cross pieces behind the seats as well as the transom plates, parts that are cosmetically visible as well as structurally vital. These originals would serve as precise templates for the replacement parts.

Removal of the electrical system and engine controls completed the disassembly process. The electrical system was a hash of pieces and parts of wiring apparently spanning the boat's entire history. It was beyond saving, much less understanding. This was discarded with the understanding that a proper wiring system would need to be professionally designed to modern needs and safety standards.

GETTING READY

As a first step, I assembled a list of the tools and supplies that I anticipated needing. I found that all of these could be purchased at Home Depot at a fraction of marine store prices. My first trip began with the purchase of supplies noted in the graphic at the end of the chapter. The tools for this part of the job consisted of a variety of scrapers, a five-in-one tool and a wooden handled hookbill knife. For the most part these were selected to cope with the variety of shapes and nooks and crannies encountered on my boat. I also received three free paint sticks which I cut in half to create 1/4- sheet sanding blocks for each grit of sandpaper.

The only tool necessary at this point, that I couldn't buy ready-to-use, was a supply of empty tin cans. The cans proved essential. The need for clean cans of different sizes was a constant throughout. In the stripping process, a clean soup can and a new brush are needed for each session as they cannot be cleaned or reused. Of course, one must ensure that expensive marine paint and varnish remains uncontaminated, and the way to do this is by dispensing small amounts into clean tin cans, which can be discarded as contaminants accumulate in the bottom. I also used cans to hold parts and clean brushes. The wonders of the can uses are endless so when you see one, wash it out and find it a job.

In order to fully assess the condition of the structure, it was necessary to strip all of the surfaces clean. Before starting, I covered the floor with cardboard to catch any drips and scrapings. I was also careful to keep the area well ventilated with a fan, and I used gloves when handling stripper gel. The stripping process was simple but slow. My method was to pour a few ounces of gel into an empty soup can and apply it liberally to a 12" x 12" area. I allowed the gel to set about 10 minutes and blister the surface. Then I simply scraped off the blistered materiel in the direction of the wood grain, and placed the scrapings into the empty metal gallon paint can. This process was repeated until the wood was clean and free of all old finish. I always let any residual chemicals evaporate over night and wiped the surface clean with a terrycloth rag soaked in VM+P naptha. This low-odor, fast-evaporating solvent will clean sanding dust from the surface of bare wood and, for a few moments, show a beautiful, clean, residue-free surface.

I quickly learned that it was essential to control the scrapings and chemicals used in the stripping process. I used empty metal paint cans with resealable tops to discard scrapings and rags until they could be properly disposed of. At the end of each day I sealed the cans and placed them either outdoors or in the middle of the floor to alleviate excess vapors and possible fire hazard. These chemical products are some of the most toxic and flammable substances available, so

before using them read the labels and instructions carefully and use manufacturer compatible products whenever possible.

In conjunction with the stripping process, I also inspected every inch of the hull inside and out. This revealed any trouble spots of dry rot in seams and ribs which would need to be addressed in the repair phase. With the surfaces completely clean inside and out, and a detailed assessment of repair needs completed, the filling and fairing could begin. Because I still had the boat on its trailer, all surfaces except the bottom were easy to access in relative comfort. With the boat completely empty it was not hard to enlist the help of eight friends and neighbors to lift the boat off the trailer and turn it over on the lawn. We then carried it back into the garage and set it on a prepared cradle of saw horses and 2 x 4s with a padded five-gallon bucket providing extra support for the bow. The hull was now in position so that the bottom could be worked on like a tabletop, ideal for stripping, sanding, filling, fairing, and finishing. With the boat upside down, the interior could also be worked on in a comfortable sitting

The hull's graceful lines are evident in this photo, which also shows the practical advantage of restoring a boat that can fit in one's garage or workspace with room to spare.

position and all scrapings and dust simply fell to the shop floor for easy cleanup.

After the bottom was stripped clean, all remnants of old marine fillers were picked out and removed from a number of scars. The original wood dough was removed from all of the fastener holes revealing still bright bronze screw heads. The worst of the seams were to the side of the keel amidships where, in some places, the seams were wide enough to pass a credit card through. For this part of the repair prep I used Git-Rot to stabilize areas with dry rot as a first step to refilling and fairing the bottom. This is a product I have used for many years with great results. A two-part product which uses a catalyst for activation, Git-Rot is mixed in small batches in its own bottle, and it reacts very quickly. After shaking briskly for about one minute, you pour the material into small holes or along dry seams where it is absorbed into wood fibers with dry rot at amazing speed, almost like water, until the area can not absorb any more. Within a few minutes the wood is as hard as epoxy and, after stabilizing for a few days, can be sanded and finished. I did learn that Git-Rot's shelf life can be a problem. I never used a package if the box had any evidence of greasy residue, appeared to be old, damaged, or on clearance sale. A bad batch can be a mess to clean up and will not perform well.

With the dry-rotted trouble areas treated, the remaining trouble spots and fastener holes were filled with Marine-Tex filler. This product is virtually underwater "Bondo", but can only be prepared in two-ounce batches, making it suitable only for small repairs. When cured, Marine-Tex can also be sanded and faired. The entire bottom was hand-sanded with small blocks fashioned from half of a paint stirring stick around which was wrapped one quarter of a sheet of sand paper. To most people this tool is absurdly small. Using it may appear to some like cleaning a floor with a tooth brush. I was often asked why I didn't use an orbital sander or a belt sander. The reason was

simple: these power tools do not conform well to subtle shapes and can cause a lot of damage to a hydrodynamic shape or surface very quickly. A boat bottom is like the aerodynamic body of a sports car. The only difference is that the dynamic is on the bottom. So if you would not use a belt sander on the fender of your Porsche, don't use it on the bottom of your boat. A boat travels on its bottom, so spend some quality time on shaping and fairing it very smooth. As the smooth coatings build up, the hull's performance through the water will be maximized.

My next step was to seal and prime the topsides and interior surfaces in preparation for finish painting and varnishing. Because this boat is made of cedar, and the entire interior would be varnished, I sealed all surfaces with Pettit Old Salem 2018 Clear Sealer. This product provides a clear amber finish that looks like varnish. It has a watery consistency and penetrates well into wood grain. It dries fairly hard and thin and, when scuffed lightly between coats, builds up quickly and provides a great base for finish varnish coats. I applied the first coat liberally until the sealer could no longer penetrate. I allowed the surface to cure for several weeks. Next, I sanded it with 150-grit sandpaper until a little wood started to come through the sealer. I then applied a second coat.

The surfaces to be painted were sanded and primed with Pettit White Undercoat. This not only acts as a primer but it also aids in filling grainy surface imperfections. The process of fairing the surfaces of the sides and the bottom, after filling and repairing, was accomplished by repeated priming and sanding of the primer. The first coat of primer revealed all of the imperfections on the surface. It was almost completely sanded off, leaving only traces of primer in the lowest spots. After washing the sanded surface with naptha, I applied a second coat of primer. The surface at this time was smooth but some imperfections were still present. I block sanded and repeated this process until the surface was completely smooth and fair, removing as much of the primer as possible with 220-grit sand paper.

Throughout this primer stage, I was careful not to allow the primer to build up too thickly on the surface. It should only build up in the low spots and when prepared for the finish coat should be as thin and even as possible, providing a clean smooth base for the finish coats of paint. The paint I selected for my finish coat was Pettit Easy-Poxy, a one-part marine paint. The repeated application and sanding of this product produces a smooth and hard high gloss finish when applied with a good quality natural bristle brush.

The issue of brushes was simple: "to clean or not to clean — that is the question." My choice was to purchase a large supply of two-inch natural bristle paint brushes of modest quality. By using a fresh brush with each application, I kept shedding to a minimum and got a clean finish. I also reduced the amount of fumes and solvents in open containers around the shop, reducing the amount of contact with chemicals as well as fire hazard. I soon learned that, because of the challenges of heat and humidity, drying and proper curing time can take longer than specified by the manufacturer. Here is where patience really pays off — building a finish from the base up by leaving longer periods of time between coats, and sanding well before recoating. If the surface pilled a little when I started to sand, I immediately stopped and waited a couple more days for the solvent to evaporate. This resulted in a hard, long-lasting finish.

With the routine of surface preparation established on the hull, my absence from many social activities drew the attention of friends and relatives. On occasion, some of my friends would push a little sand paper around or strip a couple of square feet of surface. But most were content to sip a few beverages and watch me carve away the crud inch by inch. The biggest help I had during the whole process came from my father-in-law, Bill Barclay, who, being an old salt and no stranger to varnish, began work on many of the removed wooden parts hanging on the rack. I found it greatly encouraging to come home to find a few more parts stripped, sanded, and sealed or varnished.

While I was grateful that most of the work on the boat involved cleaning and refinishing, a few parts needed to be replaced. These included the rotted cross pieces — which both brace the hull and support the backs of the seats — and the plates on the inside and the outside of the transom. These were rotten or had been roughly repaired. All these original parts had been made from oak or pine. For both aesthetic and strength reasons, I decided to use mahogany for the replacements. Mahogany was also a better match for the gunwales and the transom. While looking for mahogany, I had the good fortune to find a great source of wood knowledge and materials in the shop of a fine furniture restorer and craftsman, Chris Sirica. Chris identified the type of mahogany I needed. After a few months looking through the stocks of his suppliers and distributors he found a great plank from which all of the parts could be fashioned with the proper grain orientation and color to match the adjacent parts. After many years of attaching accessories, switches, and compasses to the dash board, I finally realized what an eye sore this key component had become. Because outright replacement would have been an extremely difficult task, I decided to place a veneer over the dashboard.

Using the old rotten cross braces and transom reinforcement parts as templates, Chris milled and shaped duplicates and fitted them to perfection. He also created a beautiful mahogany veneer for the dash board, sure in the knowledge that all of the pieces would match as naturally as the originals when installed and varnished. After filling old holes and redrilling, I would replace proper accessory switches and gear. Chris's bill for $300.00 in materials and time was very modest. I am sure that the estimate and charge for this work is a reflection of his love for the proper preservation of antique woodwork and his desire to make a unique contribution to the project.

With the hull now almost completed, it was time that I became reacquainted with all of the little bags of bronze pieces and parts so carefully sorted and stored away four years before. The parts for the decorative windshield and other gear had not been polished or cleaned for many years and were quite green with oxidation. After a brief attempt to work on the parts with steel wool and a variety of other cleaning compounds, I realized that it was going to be very difficult to clean these parts and polish them to an acceptable finish. The solution came from the most unlikely source. After consulting with restoration specialists and boat maintenance specialists, the answer to my problem came from an infomercial for Restore 4. This product is advertised to clean surfaces of tubs and tile, removing lime scale, mildew, and oxidation, with no reference to use on boats. What caught my attention was when the spokesperson dipped a 50-year-old brass or copper drain pipe, still attached to an old sink, in the solution and it came out completely clean. Wow! I unfortunately had to sit through the entire presentation again to see the trick and ordered the product. When it arrived, I poured some into a glass dish and dropped in a few screws. Presto! In a few seconds their original color was restored.

Every piece of bronze hardware went into that soup and was rinsed with cold water. In about three hours the contents of all of the bags looked incredible. The parts were so clean that it was almost six months until enough oxidation could build up to use Never Dull polish on it and raise a proper shine. For old nasty brass or bronze hardware cleanup, this was the best discovery I have ever made and will always be fondly remembered as a miracle cure.

The last phase in the project was to create a new 12-volt electrical system and wiring harness to control the running lights, compass light, two bilge pumps, and accessory socket. It was my desire to create a neat harness that would be as hidden as possible considering the boat's open design. In determining the requirements and design of the system, I invited my friend Eugene Somolowitz, a master mechanic and wizard of all things that float, fly, or roll, to see the boat that he had been hearing about for years. It was love at first sight. He sketched out a rough diagram and a parts list to accommodate all of the functions that were specified. He included accommodation for other functions should the need arise later.

While the boat was still upside down, the fuse panel was attached to the underside of the foredeck behind the instrument panel. All of the wire attachments were sealed and run to the switches, already located and installed in the dash board. They were bundled into a harness and run, with some excess wire, to the areas where the accessories would be wired later. With this stage completed, and the problems of difficult access to the underside of the bow area eliminated, it was time to call all of my friends and neighbors to turn the boat over and put it back on the trailer. Then, the final reassembly could begin.

Before this was done, however, the trailer was cleaned and primed and given a fresh coat of paint. I also purchased new tires, bearings, lights, and a winch. With the boat back on the trailer, the last of the finish coats of paint and varnish went along very quickly. Installation of seats, floorboards, supports, and hardware seemed to transform the boat drastically every day, and suddenly I found myself with the end in sight. The seats and all of the structural accessories are fastened with large bronze screws and went back together in about one day. The installation of the decorative hardware and small cosmetic adjustments also took one day. Because the electrical system was mostly complete, attaching and properly sealing the connections to the bilge pumps, lights, motor, and accessories rounded out another day.

It was now time to select and purchase the perfect motor. After many years of experience with a variety of motors on many different kinds of boats, I had formulated an ideal of what features would be required for the new outboard. Because the boat had always been used regularly and would continue to be used as often as time and opportunity allowed, the most important requirements would include dependability, power, and fuel efficiency. My experiences with antique motors are not the stuff of nostalgia, so I focused more on function than on historical authenticity. I did not intend to spend any more frustrating days with a broken-down outboard nor did I want to spend endless hours hunting for parts. Given my many years of experience at sea, I knew that the frequency of engine failure is far greater than that of sinking, and that more good days afloat have been ruined by the former than the latter. For me, using the boat means a daily run of four to six hours exploring miles of waterways, fishing and watching wildlife, or pulling up to a sandy island. In short, the novelty of antique boating for me lies in the boat itself, not what is pushing it.

I determined that the best power configuration and weight of the perfect motor was to be found in the 2003 four-stroke, short-shaft Mercury 25. This is the largest investment I have in this project — at a cost of $4,000 — which included the motor, throttle, battery, and a pair of six-gallon steel gas tanks. The last step was to run the throttle assembly and attach the motor itself. This also took one day, and with a quick flick of the ignition key, the sound of life echoed through the garage. Five years of work came to an end. In that moment I realized that the only tasks left to accomplish were registration of boat

and trailer and setting a date to launch. This was completed in late February of 2003, so I called my father to see when he might be able to escape the winter cold of New Hampshire for a couple of weeks.

My plan was to have my father in Florida for his 70th birthday, and to dedicate and launch the boat as a surprise. I decided to rename the boat *Happy Jack* in his honor — in memory of the many hours over many years that we had spent aboard. I am sure that the years of vague progress reports had convinced him that the boat would probably never be completed during his lifetime. However, when dad arrived on his birthday, April 7th 2003, the finished project was

A four-stroke Mercury has proven to deliver quiet, efficient, and effortless performance while eliminating the reliability concerns that may be involved with an antique outboard.

Ken (left) and Jack Deady pose together with the boat that has become a family tradition.

the engine burns about one gallon per hour, with a capacity of 10 to 12 gallons of fuel. It will not run out of gas on a typical day. The engine is almost silent at idle and has almost no exhaust odor. Since the boat was launched in 2003, I have logged a few hundred hours of trouble-free cruising. Given the low performance demands of the boat on the engine, I expect to enjoy it for many years to come.

IN RETROSPECT

Looking back on the time and challenges involved in this project, I can honestly say that at no time did I ever feel that it might not be worth it. The time spent doing the work was just as rewarding in its own way as the time I have spent on the water. It could not have turned out better. By following the steps and organization set out in the game plan, progress was rewarded in the results and not in the hours spent. Some of the steps involved hundreds of hours of tedium, and other steps moved the project along in great leaps. I am sure the longer hours and greater attention to prep work saved me many times from rework and mistakes. They afforded me the time to focus on problems and examine a variety of solutions to problems, letting me move forward with the best.

Many happy hours were spent in the garage with friends sharing a few beverages and doing a little work, contemplating solutions to problems, relating experiences and memories, or just watching the paint and varnish dry. The scene in the garage since completion is a change from the years of refinishing. The scene has changed from workshop to trophy room since the removal of tools, paint, and dust, and the addition of carpet and chairs. Instead of leaving for work and looking

unveiled to his great surprise and pleasure. He was speechless. I then arranged a ladder so we could climb aboard. There we sat and spent a happy hour discussing plans for the next day's cruise. Surrounded by fresh varnish and gleaming bronze, we shared a moment of mutual pride in the heritage and tradition of our boat. On that day, we began another 35-year chapter in boating tradition on the now 70-year-old Old Town Ocean Boat.

The next day, we got to savor the results of all the work. The 160-pound motor balances the boat perfectly while providing plenty of clean, quiet, and efficient power. The motor is fitted with an 11" x 4" four-bladed stainless steel prop that combines a good blend of power and efficiency at lower rpm and also acts as a governor to limit top speed. A stingray fin reduces cavitation. The Old Town now cruises comfortably at 15 knots with a top speed of 25 knots. At average cruising speeds

at my second job, I am greeted by an icon of my childhood and family tradition in pristine condition, ready to go for a ride on my next day off. All in, all the total investment in materials and services was about $2,000 over five years. The total project receipts came to $6,000.

I feel this investment was worthwhile for a number of reasons, including the emotional considerations of family history and the practical considerations of the boat's value. The appraised replacement value of the boat, in the condition it was received by me for restoration, was $4,550. This was based upon age, construction, apparent condition, equipment, and a comparison to boats of similar age. With a purchase price of $1.00, I have achieved a level of value that would allow me to get some of my investment back if I was forced to sell the boat. The boat, in its current restored condition, has generated serious offers in excess of $12,000, which I find quite flattering. But I believe a boat is only worth what someone is willing to pay for it on the day that you need to sell it. This comfort is only a validation that I did the right things in the right way to the right boat.

THE BOAT TODAY

The boat today sees regular use in the intracoastal waterway, Tampa Bay, and the Gulf of Mexico around St. Petersburg, Florida. The overall performance of the boat is great. With a quiet and comfortable ride and average cruising speed of 15 miles per hour, the boat is at home in these warm, calm and clear waters. The boat can be launched and retrieved in minutes by one person and is ideal for short runs of a couple of hours or overnight camping on local sandy islands. Cleaning and maintenance after each use protect the boat from the ravages of salt water; this is an easy and enjoyable routine comfortably completed in less than one hour. A little light polishing of the bronze accents a day before launching is guaranteed to keep heads turning. A day of boating on *Happy Jack* is usually spent satisfying the curiosity of other boaters as to the origin and age of the

The clear, shallow waters around St. Petersburg, Florida, offer Happy Jack *seemingly endless potential for day cruising explorations and the occasional camp-cruising adventure.*

boat, or having people anchor and spend a happy hour taking pictures. Whatever the weather, it is always fun. With a new lease on life *Happy Jack* is now in its fourth generation of service in our family, teaching the basics of seamanship and boating courtesy as well as providing a unique experience for old friends and new.

BOAT SPECS

Brand	Old Town
Model	Ocean Boat
Year Built	1933
Length x Beam x Draft	16' x 5' x 1'6"
Construction	Cedar strips over oak ribs
Approx. Weight	445 lbs.
Engine	25 hp Mercury 4-stroke outboard motor
Advertised speed	32 mph
Prop	4-bladed, 11" pitch, stainless steel
Original list price	$3,047
Purchase price 1967	$2,500

MATERIALS USED
- 3 gallons of KS-3 Premium Stripper Gel
- 12 cheap 2" natural bristle "bar-b-que" brushes
- 2 quarts of VM+P naptha
- 2 dozen terrycloth towels
- 2 pairs of cotton gloves
- 1 pair of jersey-lined rubber work gloves
- 2 empty gallon paint cans
- 1 package each of 80-, 150-, and 220-grit sandpaper
- 2 5-gallon buckets with sealable lids

About the Author: "I have never lived more than ten minutes drive from any ocean," reports Ken Deady, "and for most of my life, I have lived close enough to walk there." Born in Beverly, Massachusetts in 1959, Ken grew up boating on the lakes and rivers of Massachusetts, New Hampshire, and Maine. "At an early age," he reports, "I was involved with boats, beginning with cleaning and detailing as well as painting and varnishing." While attending college in Bristol, Rhode Island in the late 1970s, Ken became acquainted with sailing and chased every opportunity to crew on anything from schooners to America's Cup yachts. He met his wife Carol through his college sailing team. After 18 years of hundred-hour weeks devoted to his consulting business, Ken decided to slow his pace and start enjoying life a little more on the shallow, protected waters around his St. Petersburg home. And that is how this story of the restoration of *Happy Jack* began.

8

The Pacemaker in the Steel Mill

BY DAVE GORDON

The company that would become known as Pacemaker was rooted in the life of Charles P. Leek and the boatyard he established on the sinuous Mullica River that winds its way out of New Jersey's Pine Barrens and empties into the shallow bays around Little Egg Harbor. Leek's family involvement with boatbuilding began in the 18th century. It was natural for Leek, called C.P., to start a yard of his own, which he did at Lower Bank, New Jersey in the years before World War II. When C. P.'s sons Jack and Donald joined him, sometime around 1959 to 1961, they began offering an expanded line of models including 29-, 33- and 40-footers. These boats were called "Pacemakers by C. P. Leek." During the company's heyday from the mid-'60s to early '70s — the last wooden model was built in 1972 — Pacemaker's workforce numbered some 1,200 employees. The boats were represented by a nationwide dealer organization. Comedian Jerry Lewis was among the owners. After the Leeks sold the company, Pacemaker continued in business until 1980 when the financial problems of the then parent, Mission Marine, forced its closure.

As anybody who lives in Pittsburgh knows, the city is a place of bridges. The bridges are most in evidence on the three famous rivers that define the city. It is at Pittsburgh that the Allegheny and Monongahela meet just below the Fort Pitt Bridge to form the Ohio River. In fact, bridges of all sorts are in evidence throughout the area. In the little mill towns that line the rivers above and below the city, bridges connect one shore to the other, often spanning railroad tracks and the few steel mills that still operate in a region once almost entirely defined by their presence.

It was on Good Friday of 1995 that I found myself crossing the Allegheny on the 9th Street Bridge in New Kensington, northeast of Pittsburgh. I was in my work van, and from my high perch in the driver's seat I happened to look down over the concrete guardrail. That chance glimpse provided quite a surprise. Below the bridge I noticed that the corrugated siding of the Riggle Steel mill had been removed. I was amazed to see a large, dilapidated wooden boat inside. "Isn't that odd," I said to myself. No more than a month before I'd had a discussion with my wife, Sheri, about my desire to find a large wooden boat to restore.

Strangely enough, my first glimpse suggested that the boat in the steel mill might be just what I desired. After crossing the bridge, I decided to get a better look and looped down under the bridge to a spot where I could see the boat's stern. I felt a slow wave of inspiration wash over me. The boat turned out to be a 36-foot Pacemaker sedan. I thought she was gorgeous with her gently curving tumble-home stern and the shape of her windows.

It's not often one stumbles upon an antique wooden boat in a steel mill but that is just where Dave Gordon, seen here, found his big Pacemaker.

I proceeded into the steel mill and found a young man driving a forklift truck. He informed me of the owner's name, and that the boat was for sale as space was needed for an addition to the mill. The driver also informed me that I could look the boat over, which I did. Typical of Pacemaker, this one was made with white oak frames and planked with 7/8-inch Philippine mahogany. The roofs and decking were constructed of 1/2-inch marine plywood covered in fiberglass cloth and resin. An 80-square-foot cockpit was separated from the main salon by a set of sliding doors. The boat was designed to sleep six in three separate areas with a full galley and head.

The lift truck operator informed me that the mill owner would be at his office the next day. He suggested that I return then and meet with him. This seemed odd to me. I recognized the owner's name — not only did he own the steel mill, but also a large trucking fleet with over one hundred well-kept rigs. All in all, the boat owner didn't sound like the type of fellow that you would just drop in on, but despite my misgivings, I found myself on his doorstep the very next morning.

There, the secretary promptly ushered me into her boss's office. I found him to be friendly and to the point. He said the boat was for sale – cheap! He said that he had owned the boat for years. He had tried in vain to have someone restore it, but no one was interested. Mr. Riggle then informed me that he was planning to drag the boat up to the trucking yard, pull the engines and generator and burn the hull. He said that if I wanted the old Pacemaker, I would have two weeks to "get it the hell out of there" for a token price of $2,000 — about what he figured the engines and generator were worth. I agreed.

This was the quickest deal I had ever made. In part, the speed of the transaction was due to the fact that my wife knew nothing of the deal — she was visiting her father in Florida for the week. I didn't tell her until she got home from her trip. She was okay with the project, knowing that my background in construction had given me most of the required skills. Sheri's only issue was one of timing; I had bought the boat just as I was to begin the construction of our new home. I promised her that I would complete our 3,000-square-foot home before any work began on the Pacemaker.

The initial task was to get the boat, as the previous owner had said, "the hell out" of its present location. This proved to be a rather daunting project in and of itself. The 36-foot boat did have a trailer made from a triple-axle mobile home trailer. Over the years, however, the trailer had sunk into the dirt and some of the tires were flat. I went out and bought a 20-ton bottle jack that I used to lift the trailer axles. I had to replace the wheel bearings and races, and reseal the tires. At this point, I felt I was ready to have her pulled only to discover that the boat was seven inches over the 13.5-foot height restriction. I had to lift the entire boat, carefully using the bottle jack and blocking, and remove some of the trailer's struts. Then I lowered the cradle down inside the trailer and remeasured. I was still an inch over the limit, but saw no problems overhead as I traced the route. Just in case, I scheduled the tow truck to make the move early Sunday morning to avoid traffic and cops.

The driver was an hour late, and it had started to rain, but his rig was one that is used for towing tractor trailers and was well suited for the job. He hooked on to the boat and delivered it to its new location — the building site of our new home — without a problem. I had just had a 450-foot lane installed on the site and the excavator was digging the foundation. He'd also made a nice level spot for the boat, and the parking area had a solid gravel base for the trailer tires to rest on. As the boat came down the country road neighbors watched in some amazement. I couldn't help but wonder if they thought we were going to live in the boat instead of a house! I then blocked the boat up on its trailer, covered it with some huge tarps, and went to work on my house. It would not be until 15 months later, in August of 1996, that I removed the tarps and began my restoration project.

I began the boat restoration feeling well prepared. I'd worked as a general contractor for 15 years and had plenty of tools and equipment. What's more, our new house had a full basement that provided plenty of workspace. I had worked on cars and had rebuilt engines in my younger days. I also had experience in wood furniture restoration. There was very little of the project's work that I could not complete myself.

Towing the old cruiser home was something of an adventure but she arrived safely. Fifteen months after purchasing the boat and finishing work on his new house, Dave Gordon began the Pacemaker's restoration.

I also had one other thing going for me — time. During the period of my home's construction, I changed jobs and had reduced contracting to a part-time basis. I was now a building construction instructor at a local vocational high school. This meant that I could take full advantage of the time off in June, July, and August through the next few years to concentrate fully on the boat. Had any one of these aspects of my life been different, this extensive project would have been much more difficult.

After uncovering the boat I did a complete survey. The roofs were good with only minor rot. There was rot in the cabin sides, cabin floors, and cockpit. At least 12 frames were broken or rotted, as were the rudder and shaft log blocks. All of the decking, the toe and spray rails, flooring, upholstery, and cabinet faces needed to be replaced, as did much of the planking above the water line. The engine beds had broken as the unsupported weight of the stern over the years had sagged. The entire bottom needed to be refastened.

I decided that I would work the project from the top down. I removed everything and anything that I could, and took the items to the basement. There I planned to work on these parts during the winters. Damage to a wooden boat isn't always out where it can be seen. As I removed ever more pieces, I discovered more and more rot. I worked at dismantling the boat all through the summer and fall of 1996. That winter I began stripping the finish off some of the interior items of the boat, and I repaired the rotten bottoms of the sliding cockpit doors that I had removed.

Some of the previous owners had taken poor care of the boat — most of the weep holes around the cabin windows were plugged with debris. This contributed to the rot in the mahogany cabin sides. During the summer of 1997, I thought I might router out the rotted sections of the cabin sides and replace them. But the damage was so extensive that I finally decided to carefully remove the entire cabin sides, use one as a pattern, and make two new ones. This method of using the old as patterns for the new worked well throughout the entire project.

The mahogany cabin sides had enough rot to warrant their removal and duplication.

One interesting thing I discovered during the cabin side replacement was that Pacemaker had built each of the cabin sides from one piece of lumber measuring 24 inches by 24 feet. Wood of this size is impossible to find without paying a fortune, so I glued up shorter and narrower pieces of Philippine mahogany using Gorilla glue and joint biscuits, clamped tightly. I had shopped around the Pittsburgh area for the wood. The cheapest price I could find per board foot was around $5.00. I was getting ready to place my order when I came across a company in the Allegheny Mountains called Forest County Wood Products. I gave them a call and learned that they had a huge supply of appropriate lumber and were selling it for $3.30 a board foot. Soon after, I made the 200-mile trip and bought most of the wood that was needed to complete the entire project.

After the glue had dried on the boards that would become the new cabin sides, I simply laid the old side over the new one, clamped it, and used a fluted router bit with a special bearing that rode on the old pattern as a guide. After the new sides were manufactured, I reinstalled the sides as quickly as possible. I was anxious to avoid the disaster of high winds that could lift the temporarily supported roofs from the boat. Had this happened, I would have burned the boat like the previous owner had suggested. I was dismayed because of all of the rot that I had discovered. That same year, I began to remove the remaining cabinetry, decking, hardware, and fuel and water tanks. I was also able to reproduce the upper and lower windshields before fall came and the boat was covered for the winter.

The fall and winter of 1997 did not stop my efforts. All of the components that I had removed were now indoors. I began working on them in the comfort of the basement. I stripped the rest of the usable interior doors and cabinetry. Then I

Here, the new cabin sides, windshield, and side decks have been installed.

The basement proved an ideal place in which to work on interior components removed from the boat. Doors, seats, hatches, and other parts were all refurbished in the comfort of the heated basement.

washed the items with trisodium phosphate to neutralize the stripper. I stained the pieces using Minwax Early American stain followed by five coats of Flagship varnish. I used the same varnish brush throughout the entire project. I chose a 2 1/2-inch sash brush with natural bristles manufactured by Purdy — at a cost of around $20.

As you use a brush the hairs split and you can achieve a smoother finish. In order for a brush to get good, it must be used many times. Always make sure you clean the brush well after every use. There are at least two schools of thought pertaining to brush care. The first entails cleaning the brush with thinner and suspending it in a can of thinner to keep it wet constantly. I feel this weakens the bristles and I didn't use that method. Instead, I thoroughly rinsed the brush several

times using mineral sprits. I then dried the brush and washed it with mild soap and warm water. I then dried the brush a second time and placed it back in the sheath it was purchased in to help retain the shape.

Another technique I learned for achieving a smooth finish was to apply the varnish in one direction and smooth once. I could look in the sheen or the reflection of the light on the surface to check for runs or dry spots. I touched these up where necessary before moving on. I suspect that many people "bruise" the varnish by introducing air bubbles into the finish. This is caused by stirring the varnish before use or by stroking it back and forth when applying it.

To avoid a film of dried varnish in the can between uses, I floated a piece of plastic wrap right on the surface of the varnish and then sealed the can tightly. At next use, just pull the wrap up and hang it on the edge of the can so that the varnish drains back into the can. You can reuse one piece many times.

Everything in the interior that was rotted was reproduced, stained, coated with West System resin, sanded at a slow speed, and then varnished. I used West System 105 resin and 207 hardener. These materials gave off low fumes. The resulting finish was clear with an easily sanded surface. I used five coats of varnish on all interior surfaces because that was the recommendation of the manufacturer for proper UV protection.

With the arrival of spring 1998, I began work on the structural parts of the boat. Once the cockpit decking was removed, it was evident that many of the boat's aft frames were either broken or rotted. The shaft struts and rudder blocks were also shot. This proved to be a problem for me, as I knew very little about the steam bending process that would be necessary to reproduce the frames. I called the only place nearby that did steam bending and was informed that the cost would be $125 per bend. I had seventeen bad frames and three of them had compound bends. I quickly added up the estimate and decided to try it myself! I looked at a couple of web sites and I talked to a friend who made the loop of fishing nets by bending thin woods. I learned that I needed a heat source, a container to generate steam, a box where the wood was to be steamed, and an adjustable jig to form the frames.

I used my gas grill for the heat source. Inside the grill, I placed a new metal gas can with a small-diameter heater hose, and this became my

New cabinetry was built for the boat based on patterns made from the originals. Each component was stained and coated with epoxy resin. Such parts are likely to be more durable and long-lived than the factory-built product.

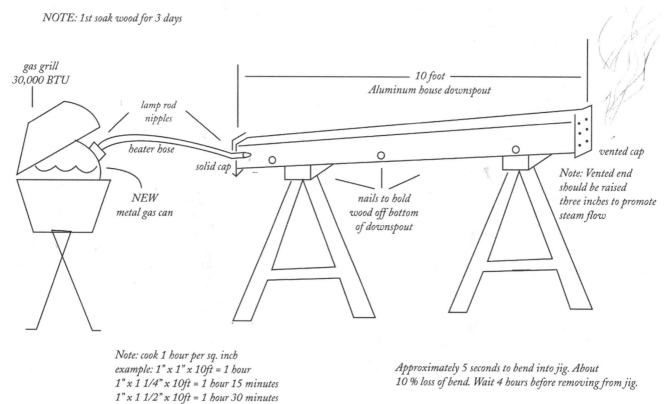

NOTE: 1st soak wood for 3 days

gas grill
30,000 BTU

10 foot
Aluminum house downspout

lamp rod
nipples

heater hose

solid cap

NEW
metal gas can

vented cap

nails to hold
wood off bottom
of downspout

Note: Vented end
should be raised
three inches to promote
steam flow

Note: cook 1 hour per sq. inch
example: 1" x 1" x 10ft = 1 hour
1" x 1 1/4" x 10ft = 1 hour 15 minutes
1" x 1 1/2" x 10ft = 1 hour 30 minutes

Approximately 5 seconds to bend into jig. About
10 % loss of bend. Wait 4 hours before removing from jig.

Here is the author's steam box apparatus. It proved entirely practical and was used to prepare the many needed replacement frames.

steam generator. The steam box itself was simply a household downspout adapted by capping it at one end, placing a vented cap at the other, and installing a fitting to take the heater hose leading from the grill. I used two pieces of plywood with blocking screwed from behind to make the adjustable jig. I then purchased the necessary white oak at the local saw mill, dressing it to 1" x 1 1/4" and soaked it in water for three days in preparation for steaming. I heated water on the grill. Steam transferred through the heater hose into the steam box where I had placed two 10-foot lengths of white oak. I let the oak cook for one hour per inch of wood thickness.

I soon learned that white oak emits a pleasant sweet smell when the wood is ready to be bent. I pulled the wood from the box and quickly bent it into the jig. Within one hour I could remove the frame and adjust the blocking on the jig for the next rib. I learned that one has around five seconds to remove the frame from the steam box and bend it in the jig before the frame becomes unworkable. There was about a 10-percent loss in the radius of the bend once the frame is sprung from the jig. I did break a couple of frames initially, but this was due mainly to the wood grain which ran across the surface of the stock rather than straight or parallel to the frame's length. It is important to select material with a straight or parallel grain.

I did the entire job for around 20 bucks instead of hundreds. I spent $8 for propane and $12 for the rough-cut oak. I replaced one frame at a time, unscrewing each plank until the frame was loose. This helped keep the boat's shape as I worked one side of the hull, then the other. I devoted the rest of the summer to replacing the frames, manufacturing a shaft log, making strut and rudder blocks, along with replacing the entire transom frame and covering it with 1/2-inch marine plywood.

During the winter of 1998 I continued to work on refinishing interior parts. I remanufactured new countertops using marine grade plywood and formica. I again used the old stuff as patterns and utilized most of the old hardware after it was cleaned up. A lot of restoration work lies in scraping and cleaning. One needs to be prepared for some tedious labor. I couldn't match hardware such as the bow chocks, anchor cleat, emblems, and stern flag base, so I took them to the chrome shop for refinishing. I purchased new foam at the local fabric store, picked out new upholstery material, and sent them out to be completed. An 82-year-old friend of mine did the upholstery work and it turned out to be exceptional. The entire job cost me about one third of what someone else

Jigs were constructed on which to bend the steamed oak frames.

New marine plywood countertops faced with formica were made using the old ones as patterns.

The original Pacemaker logos were beautifully refinished and chromed.

might have charged, but I never depend on having items like this done when promised. From experience, I know you should try to do these things early on so you will have them when needed. Murphy's Law must always be considered with a project like this.

Spring of 1999 came and I started the extensive re-planking of the mahogany hull. With solid frames in place, the planking was fairly easy. I removed one plank at a time and took it to the basement. There, I used the plank as a pattern, making sure the new plank was slightly larger than needed. The new plank was then shaped to the exact size using a joiner and a belt sander. Vertical seams on planking are located between the frames and supported by a butt block that fits snugly between the frames themselves. The ends of the planking are joined to the butt block using countersunk bronze screws and 3M 5200 sealant and adhesive.

As each plank was screwed to the frame, it was easily drawn to the correct shape of the hull. The corners of the plank were invariably higher than needed. I rounded them after installation. I used a portable planer to knock down the corners

Many of the Pacemaker's mahogany planks needed to be replaced. Each old plank was removed and used as a pattern for the new one, a process that went smoothly. The new planks were left slightly oversize and then shaped to final dimensions with a joiner and belt sander.

The screw holes in each plank were filled with a pre-cut mahogany plug set in place with waterproof glue.

and then smoothed them with a belt sander. Of course, every screw head was filled using a pre-cut mahogany plug, secured with waterproof glue. I aligned the grain of the plug with the grain of the plank. This is especially important when the finish is to be bright, but it also helps the plug to disappear after being sanded flush and painted. Ultimately, I found that about 25 percent of the planks needed replacing. Although I had recognized initially that the boat's bottom would need to be refastened, I wound up refastening the entire hull, usually driving the new screws between the two existing ones at each frame.

During the winter of 1999, I completed the rest of the varnish and cabinetry work in my basement. In the spring of 2000, I was finally beginning to see the light at the end of the tunnel. I installed the patterned 3/4-inch marine plywood decking for the cockpit. I sanded and stained the interior bulkheads of the boat. I coated everything with West System and

five coats of varnish. That summer, I spent three 40-hour weeks replacing 85 damaged acoustic ceiling tiles throughout the boat's interior and cockpit area. When the new tiles were in place, I painted them.

By September of 2000, my priorities turned to the running gear. A couple of years before I had tested both Chevy 327 engines. They ran, but I wasn't impressed by their performance. Since I had gone all out with the rest of the boat, I decided to totally rebuild the engines, or possibly replace them. I called a local tree service with a crane truck and had them lift the engines out of the boat. I had previously set up brick scaffolding over the engine well. With a stout bar across the scaffold and an electric hoist we lifted each engine onto a pallet. The crane effortlessly lifted them off the deck and placed them on a makeshift cart that was then wheeled into the basement. There we broke down the engines. We sent the blocks and cranks to a local speed shop for evaluation.

The engines were boiled and magna-fluxed, a

An electric hoist was used to remove the Pacemaker's twin engines.

The two 327 cubic-inch Chevrolet V-8 engines were totally rebuilt.

process that checks for cracks. Both engines were deemed suitable for rebuilding and the speed shop did the machine work, ordered all of the necessary parts, and printed a specification chart for assembly. During that winter, I had rebuilt the fresh water pumps, fuel pumps, alternators, and the starters. I had someone else rebuild the carburetors and secured two sets of new 350 Chevy heads. These heads were mandatory, as the old heads and valves required leaded

When the Pacemaker's engines were rebuilt, new cylinder heads replaced the originals so that lead-free gasoline could be used.

fuel. I didn't want to use a lead additive every time I fueled up. A buddy of mine had a couple of used matched sets that I traded for a day of work on his house. I had a valve job done on the heads and, when the speed shop completed the work, I assembled and painted everything without a hitch. One nice thing about Chevy V-8 engines is that parts are readily available and are very interchangeable through the model years.

January of 2001 marked the fifth year of the project and the year in which the engines were reinstalled, the boat rewired and re-plumbed. I used hundreds of feet of 14- and16-gauge stranded wire, isolating every circuit and connecting them to bus bars and fuse blocks. All of the faucets were disassembled and rebuilt. All supply lines were replaced and a new water heater was installed. The water heater I chose was a Force 10 that works either off electricity or from engine heat produced via a heater hose.

The next phase of the project was to remove all of the old caulking that remained in the seams of the original, undisturbed planking. At first I attempted to remove it by hand, but the task was daunting. So I purchased a cutting tool used for drywall work. Using some coarse bits, I was able to run the tool along the seam as it grooved out the old caulking. This made short work of a messy job. I was able to reseal the entire boat using Boat Life caulking and a household caulking gun.

With the caulking complete, I employed five of my buddies to belt sand the entire outside of the hull. I called it Sand Fest 2001. We completed the job in two days. I then applied a coat of West System and sanded the

Here, the replanked hull has been caulked and awaits painting.

finish smooth. As the winter of 2001-2002 approached, I began to install the flooring in the cabins and the salon. I purchased a commercial vinyl for the interior and Nautolex for the cockpit. Because both these products are installed with a temperature-sensitive adhesive that is spread out on the subsurface, I had to wait until the weather was warm enough to do the floors. I covered the boat with 4 mil. plastic and a good tarp. In order to complete other tasks during the winter, I rigged

Installing the Nautolex flooring represented a big step towards completing the boat's interior.

up temporary lighting and bought two ceramic heaters. This enabled me to work the whole winter inside the boat installing doors, cabinets, countertops, windows, and lighting fixtures.

By the spring of the 2002, all that was left to complete was the exterior finish. The cabin sides were varnished first. That way, if I had spilled paint, the varnish would prevent the paint from soaking into the bare wood. I used seven coats of Flagship varnish, lightly sanding the first coat with 220-grit paper. I sanded coats two through five with 320-grit paper. The last two coats were sanded with #0000 steel wool. After a week or two of drying time, I applied a coat of Johnson's paste wax.

The main hull was painted with two coats of white Sherwin Williams Tile Clad, a two-part, marine industrial epoxy. This stuff is incredible! I applied it with a low-mat roller and it dried to a smooth, glossy, and super hard shine. Because the entire outside of the boat was coated with West System, there was no need for a primer. I did the roofs of the cabins and much of the interior with Tile Clad, but in a bright green color called Circuit Breaker. I choose Interlux V-C 17 for bottom paint because of its copper color and its low ablative qualities. No boat, in my opinion, is complete without a nice red boot stripe. I installed mine after the bottom paint had set. As the old water line had been scribed deep into the wood, the boot-top stripe was easily positioned. When all of the painting was completed, I installed the chrome, stainless trim, cleats, navigation lights, and other exterior items.

Before I had the boat trucked down to the nearby Allegheny River, I wanted to insure it, so I called a marine surveyor. Now, for the first time, my work

In the slings — here is the Sheri Lin *on launching day.*

This time he arrived promptly at the appointed hour and hauled the boat down to the river without a problem.

Once at the marina, the boat was lifted by a crane into the river where it hung on the straps. This allowed the wood to swell and within two days the boat was lowered the rest of the way into the water. The next few days were used to test the engines and other systems. A sticking float on one of the carburetors and a leaking seal on a water pump were the only problems. Those bugs were quickly worked out. We then christened the boat *Sheri Lin* and began plying the local waters.

would be judged by an objective and professional outsider. The survey stated that the restoration was of museum quality and I felt that my years of efforts had been rewarded. I called the same tow truck driver who had brought the boat home from the steel mill beneath the bridge six years earlier.

IN RETROSPECT

This restoration project took six years and about $20,000 to complete. I had estimated the project to take three to four years and cost $10,000. During those years, I worked on this boat every day. Some days in the summer, I worked from morning to night. I worked on the boat Thanksgiving, Christmas, Easter, and every holiday throughout the year. We did go on a week vacation once, but it was hard for me to relax. I had a vision of the end product — I knew what I wanted — so I made it happen. It is amazing how we are all able to climb to a higher level when called upon to do so.

There were very few low points involved in this rebuild because I accomplished most of the work myself. I always tried to do my best and I was satisfied with my efforts. Most problems arose

Afloat at last — 40 years after Dave Gordon's Pacemaker Sea Skiff was built in New Jersey in 1962, the boat began a new life on the Allegheny River.

Classic Pacemakers like this were, in their day, considered generally comparable to Chris-Craft models. The last wooden Pacemaker was built in 1972, a decade after the boat that would become the Sheri Lin *was first launched.*

from work that had to be sent out. Things get lost or cost more than they should. But that's just the nature of the beast, so I learned to deal with it. The high points of the job occurred daily, as more of the thousands of pieces came together. My advice to anyone doing a similar project is: try to smell the flowers along the way.

Not all of us would want to do a project as large as mine, and that's just fine. With the experience behind me, I would recommend that anyone restoring a wood boat should choose a well-known maker recognized for building a quality product. Such a boat will, I think, be worth more when restored. My Dad always told me that you put the same amount of time and money into a car, whether you restore a Packard or a Plymouth. This rule is also true with boat restoration. Of course, this is not to say that one job or the other will offer you less enjoyment and pride when completed.

After the boat was launched in August 2002, my wife and I enjoyed it all summer long. Since then we constantly have people over for rides, which we call charters. My friends and I fish in it at night on a regular basis. We have taken it on long weekend cruises upriver to tie up to Murphy's Island. There we fish and relax.

A couple of small things have gone wrong with the boat — like losing a tiny screw from the throttle control — but I know every square inch of the vessel and the problems are readily solved. I added a swim platform, an anchor pulpit, and a good stereo system to make things more pleasant. All this effort was unexpectedly jeopardized by Hurricane Ivan in September of 2004. The storm blew straight up the Ohio and Allegheny Rivers, carrying seven to eight inches of rain. As water levels rose in the Allegheny, a dock to which four houseboats were moored broke loose. On their way to destruction at Lock #3 on the Allegheny River, the boats struck the *Sheri Lin*. Seven frames were broken, a small hole was punched in a plank above the waterline, and the rudders and props were damaged. It could have been much worse. One of our mooring cleats was partly ripped out, leaving the Pacemaker on the verge of joining the houseboats on their final journey downriver. Now that the damage has been repaired and the boat is totally complete, I am happy to have had the experience of restoring her. I learned a lot from others and my skill level has increased greatly. I have a beautiful boat that I will use for the rest of my boating career. It just doesn't get any better than that.

BOAT SPECS

Brand	Pacemaker
Model	Sea Skiff
Year Built	1962
Designer	Dave Martin
Length x Beam x Draft	36' x 12' x 2'5" (41 foot LOA with pulpit and swim platform)
Construction	7/8" Philippine mahogany planking over oak frames
Approx. Weight	12,600 lbs. dry
Engine	Two 327 Chevy 220-hp engines with straight shafts
Tankage	Two 100 gallon fuel tanks; One 60 gallon water tank (Monel)
Propellers	Three-blade, 18 x 18
Total cost	Approx. $20,000

KEY TOOLS

- Porter Cable palm sander
- Ryobi detail sander
- Porter Cable plunge router
- Table saw
- 6" jointer
- Portable planer
- C-clamps
- Bar clamps
- Parallel clamps
- Circular saw
- Mechanics tools
- Belt sander
- Saber saw
- 14-volt cordless drill
- 1/2" variable speed drill
- Biscuit cutter
- Brick scaffolding

KEY MATERIALS

- Philippine Mahogany
- White oak
- Silicon bronze screws
- Boat Life Caulk
- West System
- Minwax stain
- Tile Clad paint
- VC-17 bottom paint
- 3M 5200 sealant and adhesive
- Z spar Flagship varnish
- Gorilla glue

About the Author: Dave Gordon was born in 1956 and grew up in the New Kensington, Pennsylvania, area. Dave acquired his first boat — a 13-foot 1952 Lyman that that was rock solid but in need of paint and varnish — when he was 18 years old. The Lyman was the first of several wood boats that Dave has owned and repaired. Other boats include a 14-foot 1953 Wolverine Salary Maker, a 16-foot 1961 Higgins utility (that he still owns), and a 28-foot 1962 Chris-Craft Cavalier. After a career spent as a general contractor, Dave is now an instructor at Central Westmoreland Career and Technology Center. Dave and his wife, Sheri, were married in August of 1991. She is a Registered Representative for Prudential Financial. Dave also has a 30-year-old son Steve, who is a chemist for a local testing facility. Besides boats, Dave enjoys deer hunting, golf, snow skiing, and motorcycle restoration.